Classics in Human Development

THE BIOGRAPHY OF A BABY

*The publishers are grateful
to the late John Holt
who suggested the first two titles
in this series*

Classics in Human Development

also in this series

THE CONTINUUM CONCEPT
by Jean Liedloff

Classics in Human Development

THE BIOGRAPHY OF A BABY

Milicent Washburn Shinn

Introduction by T. Berry Brazelton, M.D.

A Merloyd Lawrence Book

Addison-Wesley Publishing Company, Inc.

Reading, Massachusetts • Menlo Park, California • Don Mills, Ontario
Wokingham, England • Amsterdam • Sydney • Singapore
Tokyo • Mexico City • Bogotá • Santiago • San Juan

Library of Congress Cataloging-in-Publication Data

Shinn, Milicent Washburn, 1858–1940.
  The biography of a baby.

  (Classics in human development)
  "A Merloyd Lawrence book."
  1. Child development. 2. Motor ability in children.
  3. Infant psychology. I. Title. II. Series.
  HQ767.9.S5 1985   155.4'18   85-21474
  ISBN 0–201–16466–3

Copyright © 1900 by Milicent Washburn Shinn.
Introduction Copyright © 1985 by T. Berry Brazelton, M.D.

Cover design by Lisa de Francis

ABCDEFGHIJ-AL-898765

INTRODUCTION

BY T. BERRY BRAZELTON, M.D.

This remarkable little book contains some of the most sensitive observations of a baby's first year that I have ever read. Toward the end of the story we see Ruth, then a year old, playing with her aunt, the observer. Aunty asks, "Where are my eyes?" and closes them. Ruth tries to find them and, unable to see them behind their closed lids, looks to the floor to see where they might have gone. What a beautiful documentation of what we now call "awareness of object permanence," written fifty years before Piaget!

Mrs. Shinn (for this is how women scholars were addressed in the nineteenth century) made her observations throughout her cherished niece's first year, documenting each new behavior in great, glowing detail. In her exuberant, warm-hearted descriptions one can see the emergence of affective, motor, and cognitive learning. Few observers are able to catch all three of these levels. Description of a single child was the method of study in that era and reminds me of the same detailed observations later made so famous by Jean Piaget.

For me, her only failing was her unwillingness to attribute experience to the newborn baby. She talks as if the newborn were an empty vessel, "gathering experiences." She describes the first two months as a "life of vegetation." Because her other observations are so keen, so insightful, it amazes me that she didn't see Ruth register recognition of visual and auditory experiences even at birth. Also, Ruth's awareness of having achieved a complex motor act—that is, combining four reflex behaviors (the tonic neck reflex, hand to mouth, rooting, and finally sucking on her fist) into a method for keeping herself under control—seems not to have been noted by this otherwise highly sensitive observer. For me, the early recognition by babies of their own ability to take in important information, or to move in a way that brings self-control, is a template for their later recognition that they can act upon their new world. This recognition then fuels them to acquire more and more important experiences. The well-equipped motor and sensory programs in newborn babies help them learn important things about their world—important to them and in setting up the patterns they will need to capture the adults around them.

In Mrs. Shinn's book, the baby's competence does not begin to surface until two months. Why was it necessary for her to think of the newborn Ruth as a recipient only? It is interesting that we now "need" to think of the baby as competent from the first—as if it were an attempt to get away from blaming the mother, who for so long was held responsible for any "failure" on the part of the baby—such as autism, a learning disability, mental retardation, or a behavior problem. All of these were blamed on the environment. Now we have developed a much more interactional approach—the baby's own qualities and reactions interact with those of the environment in order to produce the outcome. This approach makes us less judgmental today, more understanding of the organically determined "strength" of the baby in shaping the environment.

Mrs. Shinn often hedges her elegant observations with such cautions as "but she means little enough by it." She leads us through various definitions of memory, from habit memory to true memory, and finally to intentionality. Although she does not attribute intentions to Ruth until the fifth month, the baby meanwhile has brought objects to her mouth for exploration, has looked for her mother's face after it disappears, waiting for it to reappear (at thirteen weeks), has explored objects and her aunt's face with both her fingers and her mouth (at four and a half months), and has even shown a "fear of the dark" and "fear of strangers" at four and a half months. Mrs. Shinn's powers of observation clearly triumph over her theories! One of the most sensitive insights in the book is her recognition of the competition that exists between hunger and the excitement of looking at and feeling objects at five months. Mrs. Shinn correctly identifies the thrill that the baby feels at that age, when the burst of awareness about her world overwhelms her desire for food.

By the time the baby is five months old, the author is willing to admit to "real" desire on the part of the baby, and shows how rapidly her interest in objects begins to unfold. When Ruth is six months old, Mrs. Shinn identifies what we now call "means-ends," "object permanence," and "imitation," and shows the baby's increasing self-awareness. Mrs. Shinn was making these acute observations and labeling them long before Piaget had described such cognitive processes. Did Piaget read her observations and learn from her insights? I was particularly impressed with Mrs. Shinn's understanding of "her" baby's pleasure in each learning step. For example, she describes the way Ruth drops things simply to "watch them fall." Descriptions like this make Ruth seem so alive!

Mrs. Shinn's book is a classic of observation. Observation—that is, watching and recording—has a long and distinguished history as a research instrument in the natural sciences. And yet there are few volumes that include such sensitivity and attention to detail as does this "baby biography." In the words of a reviewer of the period, Mrs. Shinn had a vital asset: "the loving, sympathetic relation with the subject, necessary for insight and yet not sufficient to obscure the judgement." It is a pleasure to read a book first published in 1900, that has obviously led us to some of our present insights.

Cambridge, Mass., 1985

THE BIOGRAPHY

OF

A BABY

BY

MILICENT WASHBURN SHINN

BOSTON AND NEW YORK
HOUGHTON, MIFFLIN AND COMPANY
The Riverside Press, Cambridge
1900

CONTENTS

THE BIOGRAPHY OF A BABY

I

BABY BIOGRAPHIES IN GENERAL

"It is a well recognized fact in the history of science that the very subjects which concern our dearest interests, which lie nearest our hearts, are exactly those which are the last to submit to scientific methods, to be reduced to scientific law. Thus it has come to pass that while babies are born and grow up in every household, and while the gradual unfolding of their faculties has been watched with the keenest interest and intensest joy by intelligent and even scientific fathers and mothers from time immemorial, yet very little has yet been done in the scientific study of this most important of all possible subjects,

— the ontogenetic evolution of the faculties of the human mind.

"Only in the last few years has scientific attention been drawn to the subject at all. Its transcendent importance has already enlisted many observers, but on account of the great complexity of the phenomena, and still more the intrinsic difficulty of their interpretation, scientific progress has scarcely yet commenced.

"What is wanted most of all in this, as in every science, is *a body of carefully observed facts*. But to be an accomplished investigator in this field requires a rare combination of qualities. There must be a wide intelligence combined with patience in observing and honesty in recording. There must be also an earnest scientific spirit, a loving sympathy with the subject of investigation, yet under watchful restraint, lest it cloud the judgment; keenness of intuitive perception, yet soberness of judgment in interpretation."

I have appropriated these words of Dr.

Joseph Le Conte because the general reader is not likely to see them where they were originally printed, in a little university study, and it is a pity to let the general reader miss so good an introduction to the subject. Not all learned men rate baby biography as highly as Dr. Le Conte does; but probably all biologists do, and those psychologists who are most strongly impressed with the evolutionary interpretation of life.

It is easy to see why one's views of evolution affect the matter. In botany, for instance, we do not think that we can understand the mature plant by studying it alone, without knowledge of its germinating period. If we omitted all study of radicle and plumule and cotyledon, we should not only lose an interesting chapter from the science, but even the part we kept, the classification and morphology and physiology of the grown plant itself, would be seriously misunderstood in some ways. So in other sciences: it is necessary to understand how things came to be what they are, to study the *process of becoming*, so to speak, before the completed result can be understood.   This is what we mean by "the genetic method" of studying a subject.

Now, in proportion as one believes that the faculties of the human mind unfold by evolutionary law, like a plant from the germ, he will feel the need of studying these also genetically.   As we find them in our grown selves, they are often perplexing.   What seems a single complete, inborn faculty may really be made up of simpler ones, so fused together by long practice that they cannot be discerned.   We know that this is the case with seeing.   For instance, we give a glance at a ball, and see its form with a single act of mind.   Yet that act became possible only after long drill in putting simpler perceptions together.   Many a test of form, turning ob-jects over and over, passing the hands round and round them, learning the absence of cor-ners, the equality of diameters, did we go

through in babyhood, many an inspection by
eye, many an exercise of memory, connecting
the peculiar arrangement of light and shade
with the form as felt, before we could " see "
a ball.   Had this been understood in Froebel's time, it would have made a material
difference in his suggestions as to sense training in earliest infancy.   So other powers that
seem simple and inborn may perhaps be detected in the act of forming themselves out
of simpler ones, if we watch babies closely
enough, and it may lead us to revise some of
our theories about education.

There are enthusiasts, indeed, who would
have us believe that child study is going to
revolutionize all our educational methods, but
those who are surest of these wonderful results, and readiest to tell mothers and teachers
what is the truly scientific thing to do with
their children, are not the ones who have
done the most serious first hand study of
children.   From indications so far, it is likely
that the outcome of such study will oftener

be to confirm some good old-fashioned ways of training (showing that they rested unconsciously on a sound psychological basis) than to discover new ways. No substitute has yet been found by scientific pedagogy for motherly good sense and devotion.

Yet the direct study of child minds does bring out some new suggestions of educational value, does give a verdict sometimes between old conflicting theories, and always makes us understand more clearly what we are doing with children. And on the purely scientific side there is one aspect of especial interest in genetic studies. That is, the possible light we may get on the past of the human race.

It has long been observed that there are curious resemblances between babies and monkeys, between boys and barbaric tribes. Schoolboys administer law among themselves much as a tribal court does; babies sit like monkeys, with the soles of their little feet facing each other. Such resemblances led, long before the age of Darwin, to the speculation that children in developing passed through stages similar to those the race had passed through; and the speculation has become an accepted doctrine since embryology has shown how each individual before birth passes in successive stages through the lower forms of life.

This series of changes in the individual is called by evolutionists the Ontogenic Series; and the similar series through which the race has passed in the myriads of ages of its evolution is called the Phylogenic.

Now, of these two versions of the great world history, the phylogenic is a worn and ancient volume, mutilated in many places, and often illegible. The most interesting chapter of all is torn out — that which records the passing over of man from brute to human, the beginning of true human reason, speech, and skill. The lowest living races are far beyond the transition line; the remains of the past can never tell us how it was crossed, for before man could leave anything more than bones — any products of his art, such as weapons, or signs of fire — he had traveled a long way from his first human condition.

But from the ontogenic record no chapter can be torn out: a fresh copy of the whole history, from alpha to omega, is written out every time an infant is conceived, and born, and grows to manhood. And somewhere on the way between the first cell of the embryo and maturity each one must repeat in his own life that wonderful transition into human intelligence. If we can thoroughly decipher this ontogenic record, then, what may we not hope to learn of the road by which we human beings came?

We must not forget that the correspondence between these life books is only a rough one. They are versions of the same world story, but they have traveled far from their common origin, and have become widely unlike in details. The baby has to take many short cuts, and condense and omit inconceivably, to get through in a few brief years a development that the race took ages for. Even the order of development gets disarranged sometimes. For instance, primitive man probably reached a higher development before he could talk than babies have to now, after ages of talking ancestry: we must not look to a child just learning to talk, to get an idea of what the minds of men were like when *they* were just learning to talk. Again, the human child is carrying on under the influence of adults an evolution that primitive man worked out without help or hindrance from any one wiser than himself; and that makes a great difference in the way he does it.

The moral of all this is that people should be very cautious indeed in drawing parallels between the child and the race, and especially in basing educational theories on them. But if one is cautious enough and patient enough, there are many hints about our race history

to be found in every nursery.   Some of these
I shall relate in the following chapters.

Most studies of children deal with later
childhood, the school years; and these are
almost always statistical in their method,
taking the individual child very little into
account.   My own study has been of babyhood, and its method has been biographical.
It is hard to get statistics about babies, scat-
tered as they are, one by one, in different
homes, not massed in schoolrooms.   Now
and then a doctor has found material for
good comparative investigations, and much
effort has been spent in trying to gather up
measurements of babies' growth; but on the
whole the most fruitful method so far has
been the biographical one — that of watching one baby's development, day by day, and
recording it.

I am often asked if the results one gets in
this way are not misleading, since each child
might differ greatly from others.   One must,

of course, use great caution in drawing general conclusions from a single child, but in many things all babies are alike, and one learns to perceive pretty well which are the things. Babyhood is mainly taken up with the development of the large, general racial powers; individual differences are less important than in later childhood. And the biographical method of child study has the inestimable advantage of showing the process of evolution going on, the actual unfolding of one stage out of another, and the steps by which the changes come about. No amount of comparative statistics could give this. If I should find out that a thousand babies learned to stand at an average age of forty-six weeks and two days, I should not know as much that is important about standing, as a stage in human progress, as I should after watching a single baby carefully through the whole process of achieving balance on his little soles.

Yet there are not many baby biographies

in existence.   There are scarcely half a dozen records that are full and consecutive enough to be at all entitled to the name, and even of more fragmentary ones the number in print as separate essays is scarcely larger.   A good many more, however, have been available in manuscript to students, and many mothers no doubt keep such little notebooks.   These notes are often highly exact and intelligent, as far as they go (I have found this especially true of the notebooks of members of the Association of Collegiate Alumnæ), and afford important corroborations here and there to more continuous records.

It was the Germans who first thought baby life worth recording, and the most complete and scientific of all the records is a German one.   The first record known was published in the last century by a Professor Tiedemann — a mere slip of an essay, long completely forgotten, but resuscitated about the middle of this century, translated into French (and lately into English), and used by all students of the subject. Some of its observations we must, with our present knowledge, set down as erroneous; but it is on the whole exact and valuable, and a remarkable thing for a man to have done more than a hundred years ago.

Perhaps Darwin, in 1840, was the next person to take notes of an infant's development; but they were taken only incidentally to another study, and were not published for more than thirty years (partly in " The Expression of the Emotions in Man and Animals," 1873, partly in a magazine article in 1877). They are scanty but important. In the interval before they were published two or three small records had been published in Germany, and at least one paper, that of M. Taine, in France.

In 1881, the first edition of Professor Preyer's " model record " was published, and before his death, in 1897, it had reached its third edition in Germany, and had been widely circulated in America in Mr. Brown's excellent translation, "The Senses and the Will," and "The Development of the Intellect." It did more to stimulate and direct the study of infancy than any other publication. It has, however, the limitations that were to be expected from Professor Preyer's special training as a physiologist, and is meagre on the side of mental, moral, and emotional development. Professor Sully's "Extracts from a Father's Diary," published in part in 1881 and 1884 and fully in 1896, is richer on these sides, and also more readable.

Within the present decade, it is worth observing, the principal records have been American, not German, and have been written by women. Outside of America, only men, usually university professors, have made extended records. Professor Preyer and Professor Sully have both appealed in vain to their countrywomen to keep such records, holding up American women for emulation. My "Notes on the Development of a Child" were published in 1893 and 1899. In 1896

appeared Mrs. Hall's "The First 500 Days
of a Child's Life," a brief record, and con-
fined to a short period, but a very good one,
and perhaps the best for use as a guide by
any one who wishes to keep a record and
finds Preyer too technical. Mrs. Moore's
"Mental Development of a Child" is quite
as much a psychological study as a record,
but is based on full biographical notes; it
will be more used by students than general
readers. Mrs. Hogan's "A Study of a
Child," 1898, is less scholarly than the
others, but has a great deal of useful material; it does not begin at birth, however, but
with the fourteenth month.

Perhaps I should say a word here as to the
way in which I came to make a baby biography, for I am often asked how one should
go to work at it. It was not done in my
case for any scientific purpose, for I did not
feel competent to make observations of scientific value. But I had for years desired an
opportunity to see the wonderful unfolding

of human powers out of the limp helplessness of the new-born baby; to watch this fascinating drama of evolution daily, minutely, and with an effort to understand it as far as I could, for my own pleasure and information. I scarcely know whence the suggestion had come; probably almost by inheritance, for my mother and grandmother had both been in somewhat notable degree observers of the development of babies' minds. But, unlike them, I had the note-book habit from college and editorial days, and jotted things down as I watched, till quite unexpectedly I found myself in possession of a large mass of data.

A few days after my own notes began I obtained Professor Preyer's record, and without it I should have found the earliest weeks quite unintelligible. For some months my notes were largely memoranda of the likenesses and differences between my niece's development and that of Preyer's boy, and I still think this is the best way for a new observer to get started. As time went on, I departed more and more from the lines of Preyer's observations, and after the first year was little influenced by them. Later, I devoted a good deal of study to the notes, and tried to analyze their scientific results.

There is one question that I have been asked a hundred times about baby biography: "Does n't it do the children some harm? Does n't it make them nervous? Does n't it make them self-conscious?" At first this seemed to me an odd misapprehension — as if people supposed observing children meant doing something to them. But I have no doubt it could be so foolishly managed as to harm the child. There are thousands of parents who tell anecdotes about children before their faces every day in the year, and if such a parent turns child student it is hard to say what he may not do in the way of dissecting a child's mind openly, questioning the little one about himself, and experimenting with his thoughts and feelings.

But such observing is as worthless scientifically as it is bad for the child: the whole value of an observation is gone as soon as the phenomena observed lose simplicity and spontaneity. It should be unnecessary to say that no competent observer tampers with the child in any way. If Professor Preyer, observing the baby as he first grasps at objects, notes down the way in which he misdirects his inexpert little hands; if Mrs. Barus keeps record of her boy's favorite playthings; if I sit by the window and catch with my pencil my niece's prattle as she plays about below — and if these babies afterward turn out spoiled, the mischief must be credited to some other agency than the silent notebook.

Even direct experimenting on a child is not so bad as it sounds. When you show a baby his father's photograph to see if he recognizes it, you are experimenting on him. The only difference between the child student's experimenting and that which all the

members of the family are doing all day with
the baby, is that the student knows better
what he is trying to find out, and that he
writes it down.

Probably women are more skillful than
men in quietly following the course of the
child's mind, even leading him to reveal himself without at all meddling with him or
marring his simplicity. It has been so in
a marked degree in the cases I have seen.
But no one who has good judgment will
allow himself to spoil both the child and his
own observation; and any one who has not
good judgment will find plenty of ways to
spoil a child more potent than observing
him.

II

THE NEW-BORN BABY: STRUCTURE AND MOVEMENTS.

" ITS first act is a cry, not of wrath, as Kant said, nor a shout of joy, as Schwartz thought, but a snuffling, and then long, thin, tearless *á—á*, with the timbre of a Scotch bagpipe, purely automatic, but of discomfort. With this monotonous and dismal cry, with its red, shriveled, parboiled skin (for the child commonly loses weight the first few days), squinting, cross-eyed, pot-bellied, and bow-legged, it is not strange that, if the mother has not followed Froebel's exhortations and come to love her child before birth, there is a brief interval occasionally dangerous to the child before the maternal instinct is fully aroused."

It cannot be denied that this unflattering

description is fair enough, and our baby was no handsomer than the rest of her kind. The little boy uncle, who had been elated to hear that his niece resembled him, looked shocked and mortified when he saw her. Yet she did not lack admirers. I have never noticed that women (even those who are not mothers) mind a few little æsthetic defects, such as these that President Hall mentions, with so many counterbalancing charms in the little warm, soft, living thing.

Nor is it women only who find the new baby enchanting — in Germany, at least. Semmig, whose "Tagebuch eines Vaters" is one of the earliest attempts at a record, is delighted even with the "dismal and monotonous cry." "Heavenly music of the first cry!" he exclaims, "sacred voice of life, first sound of the poem of a heart, first note of the symphony of human life, thou echo of God's word! What sound is like unto thee?" "Yes, it is so: the cry of the baby is music! When it is still, especially in the night, one is uneasy; one longs for this primitive expression of the little being, and is consoled, enraptured, when the helpless creature breaks into loud wails, and says to us: I live, give me what I need! Oh, cry of the baby in the night, nightingale song for mother and father!"

Our baby was at least a handsome one from the doctor's point of view, strong, healthy, and well formed; and this is to be taken into account as a determining factor in all the record that follows.

I thought that she must be out of the normal in the matter of legs, so oddly brief were the fat little members. Afterward I learned that all babies are built that way — and indeed that they are altogether so different in structure from the grown man that Dr. Oppenheim, in his book on "The Development of the Child," comes near to saying that we must regard the infant as a different animal form from the adult, almost as the caterpillar is different from the butterfly.

Common speech recognizes this in the case of several of the higher animals, naming the young form as differently as if it were a different species. We say a colt, a calf, a puppy, a baby; not a young horse, cow, dog, or man.

We call a baby a little copy of the man, but really if he were magnified to man's size and strength, we should regard him at first glance as an idiot and monster, with enormous head and abdomen, short legs, and no neck, not to speak of the flat-nosed, prognathous face; and on the other hand, a baby that was really a small copy of man's body would seem positively uncanny. We see this in old pictures, where the artist tried to depict babies by placing small-sized men and women in the mother's arms.

The middle point of the baby's length falls a little above the navel, the abdomen and legs together making up a little more than half the whole length; in the man the legs alone make a trifle more than half. In proportion to the baby's total weight, its brain weighs seven times as much as a grown person's, its muscles little more than half as much.

" The two [man and baby] do not breathe alike, their pulse rates are not alike, the composition of their bodies is not alike." The baby's body at birth is 74.7 per cent. water, ours 58.5 per cent. It is largely due to its loose, watery structure that the baby's brain is so heavy — which shows the folly of trying to compare mental powers by means of brain weights, as is so often done in discussing woman's sphere. As Donaldson says, if there were anything in that basis of comparison, the new-born baby would be the intellectual master of us all. The baby has bright red and watery marrow, instead of the yellow, fatty substance in our bones; and its blood differs so from ours in proportion of red and white corpuscles and in chemical make-up as to "amount almost to a difference in kind," says Dr. Oppenheim, who adds that such a condition of marrow or blood, if found in a grown person, would be considered an indication of disease.

The organs are differently placed within the body, and even differently formed. The bony structure is everywhere soft and unfinished, the plates of the skull imperfectly fitted together, with gaps at the corners; and it is well that they are, for if the brain box were closed tight the brain within could never grow. Surgeons have lately even made artificial openings where the skull was prematurely perfect, to save the baby from idiocy. The bony inclosures of the middle ear are quite unfinished, so that on the one side catarrhal inflammations from the nose and throat travel up to the ear more readily than in later life, while on the other side ear inflammations are more likely to pass into the brain. The spine is straight, like an ape's, instead of having the double curve of humankind, which seems to be brought about by the pull of the muscles after we have come to stand erect.

I have quoted these details from Oppenheim, and from Vierordt's and Roberts's measurements, as given by Dr. Burk (" Growth
of Children in Height and Weight.")   Some
of the figures are given otherwise by other
authorities.   I might fill many pages with
similar details.   Some of these differences
do not disappear till full manhood, others
are gone in a few weeks after birth.   And
in them all there is so constant a repetition
of lower animal forms that anatomists are
brought to a confidence in the " recapitula-
tion doctrine," such as they can hardly give
to others by means of a few sample facts.

The most curious of all the monkey traits
shown by the new-born baby is the one investigated by Dr. Louis Robinson (" Nineteenth
Century," November, 1891).   It was suggested by " The Luck of Roaring Camp."
The question was raised in conversation
whether a limp and molluscous baby, unable
so much as to hold up its head on its helpless
little neck, could do anything so positive as

to "rastle with" Kentuck's finger; and the more knowing persons present insisted that a young baby does, as a matter of fact, have a good firm hand-clasp. It occurred to Dr. Robinson that if this was true it was a beautiful Darwinian point, for clinging and swinging by the arms would naturally have been a specialty with our ancestors if they ever lived a monkey-like life in the trees. The baby that could cling best to its mother as she used hands, feet, and tail to flee in the best time over the trees, or to get at the more inaccessible fruits and eggs in time of scarcity, would be the baby that lived to bequeath his traits to his descendants; so that to this day our housed and cradled human babies would keep in their clinging powers a reminiscence of our wild treetop days.

Dr. Robinson was fortunate enough to be able to test his theory on some sixty babies in the first hours of their life, and was triumphantly successful. He clasped their hands about a slender rod, and they swung from it like athletes, without apparent discomfort, by the half minute; many of us grown people could not do as well. Such a remarkable power of hands and arms has for ages been of no especial use to the human race, and it fades out in a few weeks, but for many months the arms keep ahead of the legs in development.

Here was not only strength of arms, but the ability to perform quite skillfully an action, that required the working together of a number of muscles to a definite end, — the action namely, of clasping an object with the hand. This is one of several actions that come ready-made to the baby at birth, before he can possibly have had any chance to learn them, or any idea of what they are for. Babies sneeze, swallow, and cry on the first day; they shut their eyes at a bright light, or at a touch. On the first day, moreover, they have been seen to start at a sound or a jar; Preyer observed hiccoughing, choking, coughing, and spreading the toes when the soles were tickled; and Darwin saw yawning and stretching within the first week, though I do not know that any one has seen it on the first day.

These movements are all of the class called reflex, — movements, that is, in which the bodily mechanism is set off by some outside action on the senses, as a gun is set off by a touch on the trigger. Thus, when a tickling affects the mucous membrane, a sneeze executes itself without any will of ours; when our sense of sight perceives a swift missile coming, the neck muscles mechanically jerk the head to one side.

We grown people have, however, a good deal of power of holding in our reflexes, — "inhibiting" them, as the technical expression is, — but the baby has none at all. If they had a highly developed reflex activity, babies would be in real danger from the unrestrained acts of their own muscles, as we see in the case of convulsions, which show reflex action at its extreme. But the actions I have mentioned are about all the reflex movements that have been noted in new-born babies, except what are called the periodic reflexes, such as breathing, the heart-beat, the contractions of the arteries, and all the regular muscular actions of organic life.

That so complex a system of movement as these periodic reflexes should be so readily touched into motion upon contact with air and food, to maintain itself afterward by the interplay of the bodily mechanism and external forces, shows a ready-made heredi-tary activity far more than the sudden re-flexes do. It does not work quite smoothly at first, however: the establishment of breath-ing, for instance, is irregular, and often dif-ficult. Even the sudden reflexes are slower and less perfect than with older people.

There is another class of movements, often confused with the reflex — that is, instinctive movements. Real grasping (as distinguished from reflex grasping), biting, standing, walk-ing, are examples of this class. They are race movements, the habits of the species to which the animal belongs, and every normal member of the species is bound to come to them; yet they are not so fixed in the bodily mechanism as the reflex movements. The stimulus to them seems to come more from within than from without — yet not from reason and will, but from some blind impulse. This impulse is usually imperfect, and the child has to work his own way to the mastery of the movements. Yet though certain reflex activities are inherited in a more highly developed condition than any human instincts, the instincts are at bottom *always* hereditary, which is not the case with the reflexes — any one may teach his muscles new reflex movements, unknown to his ancestors. A musician does it every time that he practices new music till his hands will run it off of their own accord, while he is thinking of something else. But instinct cannot be thus acquired.

The amazing instincts of the lower animals; the imperfect and broken condition of the instincts in man, yet the deep hold that they have on him; the mingling of inherited necessity and individual freedom in the way in which they are worked out; the mystery of the physiological method by which they act (while that of reflex movement is fairly well understood, up to a certain point); the light they seem always about to shed for the biologist on the profoundest problems of heredity, and for the philosopher on those of free will and personality,—these things make instinct one of the great fields of present research, and I must not venture into it, though it is of importance in trying to understand a baby.

I shall say only that while instinct does not appear in the lowest animals (whose action is all of the reflex type), and is for a time a sign of rising rank in the scale of life, it reaches its culmination with the insects, and as we approach man it is the breaking up of the instincts that is in its turn a sign

of advancement to higher life. The little
chicken runs about as soon as it is out of its
shell, and even the monkey baby is able to
take care of itself in a few months. Nothing
is so helpless as the human baby, and in that
helplessness is our glory, for it means that
the activities of the race (as John Fiske has
so clearly shown) have become too many,
too complex, too infrequently repeated, to
become fixed in the nervous structure before
birth; hence the long period after birth before the child comes to full human powers.
It is a maxim of biology (as well as the frequent lesson of common observation) that
while an organism is thus immature and
plastic, it may learn, it may change, it may
rise to higher development; and thus to infancy we owe the rank of the human race.

The one instinct the human baby always
brings into the world already developed is
half a mere reflex act — that of sucking. It
is started as a reflex would be, by the touch
of some object, pencil, finger, or nipple, it

may be, between the lips; but it does not act like a reflex after that. It continues and ceases without reference to this external stimulus, and a little later often begins without it, or fails to begin when the stimulus is given. If it has originally a reflex character, that character fades out, and leaves it a pure instinct.

These two types of automatic movement (for instinct, however complicated later with volition, gives rise in these earliest days to none but automatic movement) are both "purposive," though not purposed — that is, they are actions that are plainly adapted to some end by ancestral intelligence or by natural selection. But there was another type of movements more conspicuous in our baby than either, and apparently quite non-purposive. From the first day she moved slightly, but almost constantly, the legs drawing up, the arms stirring, the eyes and head rolling a little. Sometimes the features were distorted with vague and meaningless grimaces. Most other observers report these movements, and inexperienced ones say that the baby "felt with his hands about his face," or " tried to get his hands to his head." Any mother may convince herself that the baby has no will in the matter by watching till he really does begin to try, weeks later, to turn his head, put his hands to his mouth, kick up his legs: the difference in the whole manner of the action is evident.

An odd explanation has been offered for these movements by Dr. Mumford, an English physiologist. He holds that they have a singular resemblance to those of swimming amphibians; that their prototype may be seen in any aquarium; they are, in short, survivals of the period long before the ape-like stage, long before any mammalian stage, when our ancestors had not yet abandoned life in the waters.

Now, although it is quite true that biologists believe that if our ancestry is traced far enough, it does lead back to the water, still it seems hardly possible that in a human baby, whose structure passed the amphibian stage long before birth, the most frequent movements should hark back to that tremendous antiquity. It is more likely that Preyer's explanation is the correct one: viz., that the movements are simply due to the rapid growth of nerve centres, which causes an overflow of nervous force to the muscles and makes them contract at haphazard. A certain regularity is given to these chance movements by the tendency of nerve impulse to flow in the same paths where it has flowed before, rather than in new ones, so that the muscles are drawn toward the position they occupied before birth. This brings the hands constantly up about the head — a fact that later has important results in development.

These aimless movements are called " impulsive " by Preyer. I have followed Bain and Mrs. Moore in calling them " spontaneous."

There were no movements beyond these three types, and therefore none that showed the least volition. Mothers often think the crying shows wish, will, or understanding of some sort. But Preyer tells us that babies born without a brain cry in just the same manner.

Mothers do not like to think that the baby is at first an automaton; and they would be quite right in objecting if that meant that he was a mere machine. He is an automaton in the sense that he has practically neither thought, wish, nor will; but he is a living, conscious automaton, and that makes all the difference in the world. And it would be a bold psychologist who should try to say what *germ* of thought and will lies enfolded in his helplessness. Certainly, the capacity of developing will is there, and an automaton with such a capacity is a more wonderful creature than the wise, thinking, willing baby of nursery tradition would be.

If mothers would only reflect how little

developed a baby's mind is at a year old,
after all the progress of twelve months, they
would see that they rate the mental starting
point altogether too high.   And they miss
thus the whole drama of the swift and lovely
unfolding of the soul from its invisible germ
— a drama that sometimes fairly catches
one's breath in the throat with excitement
and wonder.

III

THE NEW-BORN BABY: SENSATIONS AND
CONSCIOUSNESS.

I HAVE said that the baby began the world
as an automaton, but a conscious, feeling
automaton. And what, then, were these
feelings and this consciousness? What was
the outfit for beginning the world that the
little mind brought with it? When I asked
such questions I was skirting the edge of one
of the great battle-grounds of philosophy.
Whether all human ideas are made up solely
from one's own experience of the outer world
as given him by his senses, or whether there
are, on the contrary, inborn ideas, implanted
directly by nature or God, — this is a question on which volumes have been written.

Did the baby start out ready equipped
with ideas of space, personal identity, time,

causation, such as we find so ineradicable in
our own minds? That is, did she see objects about her, located in space, nearer and
farther, right and left, and all outside and
separate from herself, as we do? hear sounds
coming from without, as we do? Did she
feel herself a separate thing from the outer
world? Did she perceive events as happening in time succession, one after another?
And did she think of one thing as happening because of another, so that, for instance,
she was capable of crying in order to cause
her dinner to be brought?

The hope of answering such questions was
the first stimulus to the study of infants, and
the earlier records are much occupied with
them. Philosophers nowadays are less disposed to think that we can prove anything
about the doctrine of innate ideas by finding whether babies have such ideas to begin
with; for we might indeed have ideas that
came direct from God, or from the nature of
the mind, and yet might not enter into our
inheritance of these at once.

To me, however, not seeking to solve philosophical problems, but only to watch and comprehend what was going on in the baby's mind, it was none the less interesting to try to make out the condition of her senses and consciousness — though without the careful special investigations certain physiologists had made before, I should have found it blind guessing as to how much she really did see, hear, and feel; for these processes, of course, went on inside her little mind, and could only be inferred from her behavior.

She evidently felt a difference between light and darkness from the first hour, for she stopped crying when her face was exposed to gentle light; and other observers confirm this. Two or three report also a turning of the head toward the light within the first week. The nurse, who was intelligent and exact, thought she saw this in the case of my niece. I did not, but I saw instead a constant turning of the eyes toward a person coming near her — that is, toward a large dark mass that interrupted the light. Either movement must be regarded as entirely instinctive or reflex. Even plants will turn toward the light, and among animal movements this is one of the most primitive; while the habit of looking toward any dark moving mass runs far back in animal history, and may well have become fixed in the bodily mechanism. With the beginning of voluntary looking these instinctive movements fade.

No other sign of vision appeared in the little one during the first fortnight. The eyes were directed to nothing, fixed on nothing. They did not wink if one made a pass at them. There was no change of focus for near or distant seeing; the two eyes did not even move always in unison, — and as the lids also had by no means learned yet to move symmetrically with the balls and with each other, some extraordinary and alarming contortions resulted.

True seeing, such as we ourselves have, is not just a matter of opening the eyes and letting the vision pour in; it requires a great deal of minute muscular adjustment, both of the eyeballs and of the lenses, and it is impossible that a baby should see anything but blurs of light and dark (without even any distinction of distance) till he has learned the adjustments. Not colored blurs, but light and dark only, for no trace of color sense has ever been detected within the first fortnight of life, no certain evidence of it even within the first year.

The baby showed no sign of hearing anything until the third day, when she started violently at the sound of tearing paper, some eight feet from her. After that, occasional harsh or sudden sounds — oftener the rustling of paper than anything else — could make her start or cry.

It is well established by the careful tests of several physiologists that babies are deaf for a period lasting from several hours to

several days after birth.   The outer tube of
the ear is often closed by its own walls, and
the middle ear is always stopped up with
fluid.   Even after the ear itself is clear and
ready for hearing, few sounds are noticed;
perhaps because the outer passage is still so
narrow, perhaps because of imperfect nerve
connections with the brain, perhaps because
sounds are not distinguished, but go all together into a sort of blur, just as the sights
do.   As the usual effect of sounds on wee
babies is to startle them, and to set off con-
vulsive reflex movements, it is well for them
that hearing is so tardy in development.

There is noticeable variation in sensitiveness to hearing, not only among different
babies, but in the same baby at different
times.   A sound that startles on one day
seems to pass absolutely unheard on the next.

In observing the sensibility to sound, one
may easily be misled.   If a baby starts when
a door slams or a heavy object falls, it is
more likely to be the jar than the sound that

affects him; if he becomes restless when one claps the hands or speaks, it may be because he felt a puff of air on his head. The tap of an ordinary call bell is a good sound to test with, causing neither jar nor air current.

Taste and smell were senses that the baby gave no sign of owning till much later. The satisfaction of hunger was quite enough to account for the contentment she showed in nursing; and when she was not hungry she would suck the most tasteless object as cheerfully as any other. Physiologists, however, have had the daring to make careful test of smell and taste in the new-born, putting a wee drop of quinine, sugar, salt, or acid solution on the babies' tongues, and strong odors to their noses, and have been made certain by the resulting behavior that these senses do exist from the first. But it requires rather strong tests to call them into action. Many babies, for instance, suck at a two per cent. solution of quinine as if it were sugar; so it seems unlikely that the mild and monotonous taste of milk, and the neutral smells by which any well-kept baby is surrounded, are really perceived at all.   There are instances related of very positive discrimination between one milk and another, either by taste or smell, shown by very young babies; yet the weight of evidence points to an almost dormant condition of these two senses.

We were told in school that the fifth sense was "feeling," but psychologists now regard this not as a single sense, but as a group, called the "dermal" or skin senses.   The sense of touch and pressure, the senses of heat and cold, and the sense of pain are the principal ones of the group.

Our baby showed from the first that she was aware when she was touched.   She stopped crying when she was cuddled or patted.   She showed comfort in the bath, which may have been in part due to freedom from the contact of clothes, and to liking for the soft touches of the water.   She responded with sucking motions to the first touch of

the nipple on her lips. Preyer found the
lips of new-born babies quite delicately sensitive, responding even to the lightest touch ;
and there are other sensitive spots, such as
the nostrils and the soles of the feet.

On the whole, however, the rose-leaf baby
skin proves to be much less sensitive than
ours, not only to contact, but also to pain,
and perhaps to heat and cold, though this
has not been so thoroughly tested. This is
not saying, of course, that the physiological
effects of heat and cold upon the baby are
unimportant.

Our baby had no experience of skin pain
in her early days, and being kept at an
equable temperature, probably received no
definite sensations either of heat or of cold.

The foregoing are the " special senses,"
that is, those that give impressions of external things, and have end organs to receive
and make definite these impressions, — the
eye at the end of the optic nerve, the different kinds of nerve tips in the skin, and so

forth.   Another sense now claims almost to rank with them,—the recently studied sense of equilibrium and motion, by which we feel loss of balance in our bodies and changes in their motion (changes only, for no one can feel perfectly smooth motion).   This sense has been traced to the semicircular canals of the ear; and as this part of the ear is the oldest in evolution, and the rudimentary ears of the lower orders of animals are quite analogous to it in structure, biologists now suspect that hearing may be a more recent sense than we have thought, and that much which has been taken for sense of sound in the lower animals — even as high as fishes — may perhaps be only a delicate sense of motion.

I failed to watch for this motion sense in the baby.   It would have been shown by signs that she felt change of motion when she was lifted and moved.   Equilibrium sense she must have used as soon as she began to balance her little head, but in the first limp

and passive days there was no sign of it.
Still, there are tales of very young babies
who showed disturbance, as if from a feeling
of lost equilibrium, when they were lowered
swiftly in the arms.

There is besides a sort of sensibility to
vibration that affects the whole body. We
know how much of the rhythm of music may
be caught quite soundlessly through the
vibrations of the floor; and it is said (perhaps not altogether credibly) that it was thus
that Jessie Brown recognized even the instru-
ments and the tune at the relief of Lucknow
by the tremor along the ground before a
sound was audible. A jar, affecting the
whole body, seems to be felt by creatures of
very low organization. Babies are undoubtedly quite susceptible to jarring from the
earliest days. Champney's baby started
when the scale of the balance in which he
was lying immediately after birth sprang up.

Then there is the " muscle sense " — the
feeling of the action of our own muscles;

and a most delicate and important sense this is. It is safe to say that the baby had it from the first, and felt the involuntary movements her own little body was making, for it is hardly conceivable how else she could have learned to make voluntary ones. But that is another story, and comes later.

Even this does not exhaust the list of sensations the baby could feel. There was the whole group of " organic sensations," coming from the inner organs, — hunger, thirst, organic pain. With older people, nausea, suffocation, choking, and perhaps some others might be added; but little babies certainly do not feel nausea, — their food regurgitates without a qualm. Nor do they seem to feel disagreeable sensations when they choke in nursing.

Organic pain our baby had her touch of in the usual form of colic; and hunger was obviously present very early, though perhaps not in the first two or three days. Thirst appeared from the first, and was always imperative. Of course, the milk diet largely satisfied it, but not entirely. Luckily our baby did not suffer from thirst, for grandma, nurse, and the good doctor had all entered early warning that "babies needed water," and that many a baby was treated for colic, insomnia, nervousness, and natural depravity, when all the poor little fellow wanted was a spoonful of cool water. The baby's body, as I said in my last chapter, is largely composed of water, and the evaporation from the loose texture of the skin is very great. After children can talk, they wear out the most robust patience with incessant appeals, night and day, for a " d'ink," and consume water in quantities quite beyond what seems rational. But their craving is doubtless a true indication of what they need.

There are composites of sensation which the baby experiences very early. There is the feeling of clothes, for instance, made up of warmth, of touch and pressure sensations

all over his skin, and of changes in the muscular feelings from constraint, and in the
internal feelings from the effect on circulation. There are feelings of fatigue in one
position, made up of sensations of touch, of
the pressure of the body's weight on the
under surfaces of skin, of some muscular
tensions, and perhaps of several other elements. Our baby's nurse saved her much
fretting by simply changing the position of
the little body from time to time. We ourselves are constantly moving and shifting
our positions, to relieve a pressure on the
skin here, or a muscular tension there, but
the wee baby cannot so much as turn his
head or move a limb at will.

Vaguest and most composite of all is what
is called "common sensation," or "general
sensation" — that feeling of comfort or discomfort, vigor or languor, diffused through
the whole body, with which we are all familiar. It seems to be very primitive in origin
— indeed, the speculation is that this dim,

pervasive feeling is the original one, the primitive way in which animal tissue responded to light and heat and everything, before the special senses developed, gathering the light sensations to one focus, the sound sensations to another, and so on. But in its present development it is also largely made up of the sum of all the organic sensations, and even of dim overflows of feeling from the special senses.

It is with older people notably connected with emotional states. It varies, of course, with health and external conditions; yet each person seems from birth to be held to a certain fixed habit in this complex underlying condition of feeling — pleasant with one, unpleasant with another. This fixed habit of general sensation is perhaps the secret of what we call temperament; while its surface variations seem to be mainly responsible for moods.

Our baby showed temperament — luckily of the easy-going and cheerful kind — from her first day (though we could hardly see this except by looking back afterward); and there is no reason to doubt that she experienced some general sensation from the first. It was evidently of a pretty neutral sort, however: the definite appearance of high comfort and well-being did not come till later; nor were moods apparent at first.

Now in all this one significant thing appears. Sensations had from the first the quality of being agreeable or disagreeable. The baby could not wish, prefer, and choose, for she had not learned to remember and compare; but she could like and dislike. And this was shown plainly from the first hour by expressions of face — reflex facial movements, so firmly associated in the human race with liking and disliking that the most inexperienced observer recognizes their meaning at once. It is said that facial expression comes by imitation, and that the blind are therefore deficient in it; but this is not true of these simplest expressions: they come by

inheritance, and are present in the first hour
of life.   A look of content or discontent, the
monotonous cry, and vague movements of
limbs, head, and features, — these are the
limits of expression of feeling in the earliest
days.

It would seem that in this sense condition
there was nothing that could give the baby
any feeling of inner or outer, of space or
locality.   We have some glimpse of the like
condition ourselves, — when people say after
an explosion, for instance, that it " seemed
to be inside their own heads," or when we
try to locate a cicada's note, or when we feel
diffused warmth.

Here is the conception I gathered of the
dim life on which the little creature entered
at birth.   She took in with a dull comfort
the gentle light that fell on her eyes, seeing
without any sort of attention or comprehension the moving blurs of darkness that varied
it.   She felt motions and changes; she felt
the action of her own muscles; and, after

the first three or four days, disagreeable
shocks of sound now and then broke through
the silence, or perhaps through an unnoticed
jumble of faint noises.   She felt touches on
her body from time to time, but without the
least sense of the place of the touch (this
became evident enough later, as I shall relate
in its order); and steady slight sensations of
touch from her clothes, from arms that held
her, from cushions on which she lay, poured
in on her.

From time to time sensations of hunger,
thirst, and once or twice of pain, made
themselves felt through all the others, and
mounted till they became distressing; from
time to time a feeling of heightened comfort
flowed over her, as hunger and thirst were
satisfied, or release from clothes, and the
effect of the bath and rubbing on her circulation, increased the net sense of well-being.
She felt slight and unlocated discomforts
from fatigue in one position, quickly relieved
by the watchful nurse.   For the rest, she lay

empty-minded, neither consciously comfortable nor uncomfortable, yet on the whole
pervaded with a dull sense of well-being.
Of the people about her, of her mother's
face, of her own existence, of desire or fear,
she knew nothing.

Yet this dim dream was flecked all through
with the beginnings of later comparison and
choice. The light was varied with dark;
the feelings of passive motion, of muscular
action, of touch, of sound, were all unlike
each other; the discomforts of hunger, of
pain, of fatigue, were different discomforts.
The baby began from the first moment to
accumulate varied experience, which before
long would waken attention, interest, discrimination, and vivid life.

IV

THE EARLIEST DEVELOPMENTS

Out of the new-born baby's dim life of passivity the first path was that of vision. I noticed about the end of the second week that her eyes no longer wandered altogether helplessly, but rested with a long and contented gaze on bright surfaces they chanced to encounter, such as the shining of the lamp on the white ceiling, or our faces turned toward the light as she lay on our knees. It was not active looking, with any power to direct the eyes, but mere staring; when the gaze fell by chance on the pleasant light, it clung there. But something must have come to pass, that it *could* stop and cling to what gave it pleasure.

I think no one has yet analyzed this earliest stage in progress toward real seeing, though Professor Sully touches on an explanation when he says that the eyes " maintain their attitude under stimulus of the pleasure."

We know that muscular action is normally caused by stimulus received from the nerve centres, and that in the earliest days there seems to be a good deal of random discharge of stimulus, developed by the growth of the centres, and causing aimless movements. Now there are two fundamental and profoundly important things about this nervous discharge. One is that pleasure, attention, or intensity of sensation seems to have the power of increasing it, and thus influencing the action of the muscles. The other is that the discharge always tends to seek the same paths it has used before, and more and more easily each time ; so that physiologists speak of it as a current deepening its channels. It is really nothing like a flowing liquid, nor the nerve threads along which it passes like channeled watercourses. Still, just as a current of water will deepen a gully till it drains into itself all the water that had spread about in shallower ditches, so the wave of molecular change running along a nerve somehow so prepares that nerve that by and by, instead of spreading about through any fibres that come handy, the whole energy will drain into the accustomed ones. Then, of course, the muscles to which these run will perform more and more easily the accustomed acts. Some of these channels — even whole connected systems of them — are already well prepared by inheritance, and hence come instinctive and reflex actions; many are still to be deepened by the baby's own experience.

Now suppose the aimless impulse straying to the baby's eye muscles, making the eyes roam hither and yon; but as they reach a certain position, they fall upon a lighted surface, and a pleasant brightness flows back into the consciousness; and something stirs within that has power to send an intenser current through those same fibres. For the time, at least, that channel is deepened, the wandering impulses are drained into it, and the eye muscles are held steady in that position. And, in fact, with the beginning of staring the irregular movements of head and eyes did decline, and gradually disappear.

It is an important moment that marks the beginning of even a passive power to control the movements; and when my grandmother handed down the rule that you should never needlessly interrupt a baby's staring, lest you hinder the development of power of attention, she seems to have been psychologically sound.

A fuller and pleasanter life now seemed to pervade the whole little body. The grimaces of vague discomfort were disappearing, and the baby began to wear a look of satisfaction as she lay, warm and fed and dry, gazing at some light surface. In the bath, where the release from clothes and the stimulus to circulation from the warm water heightened the pleasant condition of general sensation, her expression approached real delight; the movements of her limbs were freer, and all her muscles tenser.

The neck muscles, especially, were so far "innervated" — that is, supplied with nervous energy — as fairly to lift her head from the supporting hand. This was probably not as yet a real effort to hold up the head, only a drafting of surplus energy into the neck muscles, partly because of inherited aptitude, partly because the pleasure received from the lifted head and better seeing tended to draw the energy thither, just as it was drawn to the eye muscles in the case of the staring. At least one careful observer, Mrs. Edith Elmer Wood, records this action of the neck muscles on the first day.

It was at this period that the baby first smiled; but being forewarned of the "colic smile," which counterfeits so exactly the earliest true smiles, — fleeting as these are, just touching the mouth and vanishing, — I

never felt sure whether the baby was smiling
for general contentment with life, or whether
a passing twinge had crossed her comfort
and drawn her lips into the semblance of a
smile; and so never dared to record the expression till it first occurred for unmistakable
pleasure.

There must have been rapid progress
going on in the clearness of muscular and
touch sensations, and in the forming of associations in the baby's mind; but no plain
evidence of these inner processes came till
the fourth week. Then I noticed that the
baby, when crying with hunger, would hush
as soon as she was taken in the arms in the
position usual in nursing, as if she recognized
the preliminaries, and knew she was about
to be satisfied. She could not, in fact, have
remembered or expected anything as yet; it
was not memory, but a clear instance of the
working of that great law of association by
which the raw material of the senses was to
be wrought up into an orderly mental life.

The substance of the law is that when experiences have repeatedly been had together, the occurrence of one of them (still more, of several out of a group, as in this case) tends to bring up into consciousness the others. It is a law that underlies psychic life as profoundly as the law that nerve energy seeks its old channels underlies physical life. Indeed, it is in a sense the psychic side of the same law; for it implies that when a group of nerve centres have formerly acted together, the action of one tends to bring on that of the rest. So, since the baby had often experienced the feeling of that particular position (a combination of tactile and muscular and organic sensations) in connection with the feeling of satisfied hunger, that comfortable feeling, the missing member of the group, came into her consciousness along with the rest, some moments in advance of the actual satisfaction.

I have said that this is not memory, yet there is in it a germ of memory. A past experience is brought back to consciousness; and if it were brought back as a definite idea, instead of a vague feeling, it would be memory.

Close on this came another great advance in vision. This was on the twenty-fifth day, toward evening, when the baby was lying on her grandmother's knee by the fire, in a condition of high well-being and content, gazing at her grandmother's face with an expression of attention. I came and sat down close by, leaning over the baby, so that my face must have come within the indirect range of her vision. At that she turned her eyes to my face and gazed at it with the same appearance of attention, and even of some effort, shown by a slight tension of brows and lips, then turned her eyes back to her grandmother's face, and again to mine, and so several times. The last time she seemed to catch sight of my shoulder, on which a high light struck from the lamp, and not only moved her eyes, but threw her head far back to see it better, and gazed for some time, with a new expression on her face — "a sort of dim and rudimentary eagerness," says my note. She no longer stared, but really looked.

Clear seeing, let us here recall, is not done with the whole retina, but only with a tiny spot in the centre, the so-called "yellow spot," or "macula lutea." If the image of an object falls to one side of this, especially if it is far to one side, we get only a shape-less impression that something is there; we "catch a glimpse of it," as we say. In order really to look at it we turn our eyeballs toward the object till the image falls on the spot of clear vision. We estimate the dis-tance through which to turn the balls, down to minute fractions of an inch, by the feeling in the eye muscles.

This was what the baby had done, and I do not dare to say how many philosophical and psychological discussions are involved in her doing it. Professor Le Conte thinks that it shows an inborn sense of direction, since the eyes are turned, not toward the side on which the ray strikes the retina, but toward the side from which the ray enters the eye ; that is, the baby thinks out along the line of the ray to the object it comes from, thus putting the object outside himself, in space, as we do. Professor Wundt, the great German psychologist, is positive that the baby has no sense of space or direction, but gains it by just such measurements with the eye muscles ; that there is no right nor left, up nor down, for him, but only associations between the look of things off at one side, and the feel of the eye action that brings them to central vision.

This means that before a baby can carry the eye always through just the right arc to look at an object, he must have made this association between the look of things and the feel of the action separately for each point of the retina. It is a great deal for a baby to have learned in three weeks ; still, babies have to learn fast if they are ever to catch up with the race; and in the early roamings of the eye they experience over and over all manner of transits of images to and fro across the retina. Probably, too, it was still only partially learned.

I watched now for what Preyer's record had led me to expect as the next development in vision — the ability to follow a moving object with the eyes; that is, to hold the yellow spot fixed on the object as it moved, moving the eyeball in time with it in order to do so. I used my hand to move to and fro before the baby, and could not satisfy myself that she followed it, though she sometimes seemed to; but the day after she was a month old I tried a candle, and her eyes followed it unmistakably; she even threw her head back to follow it farther. In trying this experiment, one should always use a bright object, should make sure the baby's eyes are fixed on it, and then should move it very slowly indeed, right and left.

So far, there is no necessary proof of will.

Longet found that the eyes and head of a pigeon whose cerebrum had been removed would follow a moving light. We ourselves can sit absorbed in thought or talk, yet follow unconsciously with our eyes the movement of a lantern along a dark road; and if something appears on the outer edge of our vision we often turn quite involuntarily to look. But the baby's new expression of intelligence and interest showed that whether she willed the movements or not, she attended to the new impressions she was getting.

Professor Preyer noticed the same dawn of intelligence in his baby's face at about the same stage. And it is worth while to observe that when I came to study my record I was surprised to find how often such an awakening look, an access of attention, wonder, or intelligence, in the baby's face, had coincided with some marked step in development and signalized its great mental importance. I should advise any one who is observing a baby to be on the lookout for this outward and visible sign of an inward and spiritual unfolding.

In both these visual developments the baby had proved able to use her neck in co-operation with her eyes, throwing back her head to see farther. It began at the same time to seem that she was really and deliberately trying to hold up her head for the same purpose of seeing better. She not only straightened it up more and more in the bath, but when she was laid against one's breast she would lift her head from the shoulder, sometimes for twenty seconds at a time, and look about. Preyer sets this down as the first real act of will.

The baby's increased interest in seeing centred especially on the faces about her, at which she gazed with rapt interest. Even during the period of mere staring, faces had oftenest held her eyes, probably because they were oftener brought within the range of her clearest seeing than other light surfaces. The large, light, moving patch of the human face (as Preyer has pointed out) coming and going in the field of vision, and oftener chancing to hover at the point of clearest seeing than any other object, embellished with a play of high lights on cheeks, teeth, and eyes, is calculated to excite the highest degree of attention a baby is capable of at a month old. So from the very first — before the baby has yet really seen his mother — her face and that of his other nearest friends become the most active agents in his development, and the most interesting things in his experience.

Our baby was at this time in a way aware of the difference between companionship and solitude. In the latter days of the first month she would lie contentedly in the room with people near by, but would fret if left alone. But by the end of the month she was apt to fret when she was laid down on a chair or lounge, and to become content only when taken into the lap. This was not yet distinct memory and desire, but it showed that associations of pleasure had been formed with the lap, and that she felt a vague discomfort in the absence of these.

Just before she was a month old came an advance in hearing. So far this sense had remained little more than a capacity for being startled or made restless by harsh sounds. I had tested it on the twenty-third day, and found that the baby scarcely noticed the sound of an ordinary call bell unless it was struck within about six inches of her ear, and suddenly and sharply at that; and on the twenty-sixth day she showed no sign of hearing single notes of the piano, struck close to her, from the highest to the lowest. But the next day, at the sound of chords, strongly struck, she hushed when fretting with hunger, and listened quietly for five minutes — her first pleasant experience through the sense of hearing.

In the following days she would lie and take in the sound of the chords with a look of content, staring at the same time into the face of the person who held her, as if she associated the sound with that. Only a few days later, when she was a month old, I thought that her pleasure in companionship was increased if she was talked and crooned to; and it is likely that by this time, though she had not hitherto noticed voices, she was beginning to get them associated with the human face — probably to the enhancement of its charm.

There were signs now, too, that touch sensations, in their principal seat, the lips, were becoming a source of pleasure. The first smile that I could conscientiously record occurred the day before the baby was a month old, and it was provoked by the touch of a finger on her lip; and a day or two later she smiled repeatedly at touches on her lip. The day before she was a month old, also, when her lips were brought up to the nipple, she laid hold upon it with them — the first seizing of any sort, for her hands were still in their original helplessness, waving vaguely about at the will of the nerve currents.

It is plain that the eyes led in the development of the psychic life. Yet the baby was still far from real seeing. Professor Preyer believes that there is at this stage no " accommodation " of the eyes to near and far, although they can now be focused for right and left: that is, both yellow spots can be brought to bear in unison on an object, but the lenses do not yet adjust themselves to different distances. Though the baby may have perceived direction, then, she could not have perceived depth in space. It was only when an object chanced to be at the distance for which her eyes were naturally adjusted that she could have seen it clearly.

Nor is it likely that even then she saw anything as a definite outline, but only as an undefined patch. The spot of clear vision in our eyes is very small (a twenty-five cent piece would cover all the letters I can take in at once on this page, if I do not let my

eyes move in the least), and the only way
we ourselves see anything in definite outline
is by running our eyes swiftly over its surface and around its edges, with long trained
and unconscious skill. The baby had not
yet learned to do this. Her world of vision,
much as it pleased her, was still only patches
of light and dark, with bits of glitter and
motion. She could turn her eyes and lift
her head a little to make the vision clearer;
but except about her neck, eyes, and in a
slight degree her lips, she had no control of
her body. She had gained much in grouping and associating together her experiences,
yet on the whole she still lived among disjointed impressions.

In the light of such interpretations, the
speculative attempts to arrange a system of
cradle education become futile. What can
a swinging ball do for a pupil whose sense
apparatus is not yet in condition to see the
outline of the ball definitely? Froebel himself could not have been expected to know

much of the condition of a baby's sense apparatus; but modern Froebelians would be better apostles of his almost Messianic inspiration if they were willing to throw frankly aside his unfounded speculations and his obsolete science. The letter killeth, but the spirit giveth life.

Meanwhile, nature has provided an educational appliance almost ideally adapted to the child's sense condition, in the mother's face, hovering close above him, smiling, laughing, nodding, with all manner of delightful changes in the high lights; in the thousand little meaningless caressing sounds, the singing, talking, calling, that proceed from it; the patting, cuddling, lifting, and all the ministrations that the baby feels while gazing at it, and associates with it, till finally they group together and round out into the idea of his mother as a whole.

Our baby's mother rather resented the idea of being to her baby only a collection of detached phenomena, instead of a mamma;

but the more you think of it the more flattering it is to be thus, as it were, dissolved into your elements and incorporated item by item into the very foundations of your baby's mental life. Herein is hinted much of the philosophy of personality; and Professor Baldwin has written a solid book, mainly to show from the development of babies and little children that all other people are part of each of us, and each of us is part of all other people, and so there is really no separate personality, but we are all one spirit, if we did but know it.

V

BEGINNINGS OF EMOTION AND PROGRESS IN SENSE POWERS

THE baby entered on her second month well content with her fragmentary little world of glancing lights and shining surfaces, chords and voices, disconnected touches and motions. Her smiles began to be frequent and jolly. It was always at faces that she smiled now : nothing else seemed half as entertaining. The way in which a baby, in these early weeks, gazes and gazes up into one's face, and smiles genially at it, wiles the very heart out of one ; but the baby means little enough by it.

In this fortnight her pleasures were enlarged by introduction to a baby carriage. The outdoor sights and sounds were of course wasted on her at this stage of her

seeing and hearing powers; but she liked
the feeling of the motion, and lay and enjoyed it with a tranquilly beatific look.   Perhaps also the fresher air and larger light sent
some dim wave of pleasant feeling through
her body.

Some days earlier, when carried out in
arms for her first outdoor visit, she had found
the light dazzling, and kept her eyes tight
shut.   In all I have said of babies' pleasure
in light, I have meant moderate light: the
little eyes are easily hurt by a glare.   There
are nursemaids, and even mothers, who will
wheel a baby along the street with the sun
blazing full in his face, and who will keep a
light burning all night for their own convenience in tending him; and in later years
his schoolbooks will get the credit of having
weakened his eyes.   Nature protects the little
one somewhat at the outset, for at first the
eyes open by a narrow slit, which admits but
scanty light: our baby was just beginning, at
a month old, to open her eyes like other folk.

Pleased though the baby was with her new powers, her life at this period was not all of placid content. Ambition had entered in. It had already seemed as if the mechanical lifting of the head was passing into real effort to raise it; and day by day the intention grew clearer, and the head was held up better. Now, too, appeared the first sign of control over the legs. Laid on her face on the lounge, the baby did not cry, but turned her head sidewise and freed her face, and at the same time propped her body with her knees. This was on the first day of the month. A few days later she was propping herself with her knees in the bath every day.

With increase of joy and power came also the beginning of tears. This, too, was on the first day of the month. The tears were shed because she had waked and cried some time without being heard. When she was at last taken up, her eyes were quite wet. As every nurse knows, wee babies do not cry tears. When they do, it does not mean that any higher emotional level has been gained, only that the tear glands have begun to act. Nor have I any reason to suppose that in this case the baby felt fear at being left alone. It was simply that she was uncomfortable, and needed attention; and the attention delaying, the discomfort mounted, till it provoked stronger and stronger reflex expressions.

The first fright did occur, however, a few days later in the same week; but it was in a much more primitive form than fear of solitude. The baby was lying half asleep on my lap when her tin bath was brought in and set down rather roughly, so that the handles clashed on the sides. At this she started violently, with a cry so sharp that it brought her grandfather anxiously in from two rooms' distance; she put up her lip at the same time, with the regular crying grimace known to every nursery,—the first time she had done this,—and it was fully five minutes before her face was tranquil again.

There had been reflex starting at sounds from the first week, and Professor Preyer calls this an expression of fright; but to me (and Professor Sully regards it in the same way) it seemed purely mechanical. Our baby would even start and cry out in her sleep at a sound without waking. But now there was clearly something more than reflex starting. It was not yet true fear, for fear means a sense of danger, an idea of coming harm, and the baby could have had no such idea. But there was some element of emotion to be seen, akin to fear; and (if we regard pleasure and pain as psychologists are disposed to do, not as emotions in themselves, but only as a quality of agreeableness or disagreeableness in our feelings) here was the first dawn of any emotion. Fright, that was but a step above mere physical shock, led the way into the emotional life.

This probably gives a true hint of the history of emotional development in the race: for in the animal world, too, fear appears earliest of all the emotions, and in the simplest forms of fright is hardly to be distinguished from mere reflex action ; and it is caused oftener by sound than by anything else. When we remember the theory that hearing is developed from the more ancient motion sense, we are tempted to trace the origin of fright still farther back, to the very primitive reflex sensibility to jarring movement, of which I have spoken before.

And now the baby had come to six weeks old, and could hold up her head perfectly for a quarter of a minute at a time, and liked greatly to be held erect or in sitting position. Apparently all this was for the sake of seeing better, for her joys still centred in her eyes. She had made no advance in visual power, however, except that within a few days she could follow with her eyes the motion of a person passing near her.

Human faces were still the most entertaining of all objects. She gazed at them with her utmost look of intentness, making movements with her hands, and panting in short, audible breaths. Nothing else had ever excited her so, except once a spot of sunlight on her white bed.

There were signs that her experiences gathered more and more into groups in her mind, by association. I have spoken of her earlier association between the nursing position and being fed; now she would check her hungry crying as soon as she felt herself lifted; and a few days later, as soon as her mouth was washed out — a ceremony that invariably came before nursing. At seven weeks old she opened her mouth for the nipple on being laid in the proper position. The food association group was enlarging; but sight did not yet enter into it: the look of the breast did not seem to bring the faintest suggestion of satisfied hunger, and the baby would lie and cry with her lips an inch from it. This is natural, for she could never really have seen it at this stage of the development of vision.

I have said that in such associations there is a germ of memory. There is a sort of habit memory, too, that appears very early. Impressions that have been received over and over gather a sort of familiarity in the baby's mind; and while he does not yet recognize the familiar things themselves, yet he feels a change from them as something strange — it jars somehow the even current of his feelings. Or where impressions have been especially agreeable, they are vaguely missed when they are absent. The consciousness of difference between society and solitude, which our baby had showed at the end of the first month, was habit memory of this sort.

Professor Preyer thinks that his baby showed habit memory as early as the first week, perceiving a new food to be different from the old. Our baby (who knew no food but mother's milk) experienced a new taste once or twice, when dosed for colic, and never showed the faintest sense of novelty at it till she was six weeks old.   Then she was given a little sugar for hiccoughs, and made a face of what seemed high disgust over it; but this particular face has been observed more than once, and is known to be common in babies at a new taste, even a pleasant one. It seems to be caused by a sort of surprise affecting the face muscles.

A few days later the baby showed surprise more plainly.   She lay making cheerful little sounds, and suddenly, by some new combination of the vocal organs, a small, high crow came out — doubtless causing a most novel sensation in the little throat, not to speak of the odd sound.   The baby fell silent instantly, and a ludicrous look of astonishment overspread her face.   Here was not only evidence of the germs of memory, but also the appearance of a new emotion, that of genuine surprise; and, like fright, it is one that is closely related to simple nerve shock.   From being startled to being surprised (as to being frightened) is not a long step.

I have just spoken of the baby as making little sounds. This was a new accomplishment. Until a few days before, she had made no sounds except some inarticulate fretting noises, the occasional short outcry when startled, and the " dismal and monotonous" cry that began with the first day. This original cry was clearly on the vowel *â* (as in fair), with a nasal prefix — *ngâ;* but late in the sixth week it began to be varied a little. In the fretting, too, a few syllables appeared. The new sounds were mostly made in the open throat, and grew out of the old *ngâ* by slight changes in the position of the vocal organs — *ng,* and *hng,* and *hng-â;* but now and then there was a short *wă, gă,* or *hă,* or even a lip sound, as *m-bă.*

It has been said that the broad Italian *ä* is of all sounds the easiest, the one naturally made from an open throat: but the records show both German and American babies beginning with the flat *â,* or shorter *ă.* Our baby scarcely used any other vowel sound for weeks yet.

Little sounds of content, too, began in the sixth week — mainly inarticulate grunts and cooing murmurs; but in the course of the seventh week, besides the sudden crow, there were a few tiny shouts, — *a-a-ha*, — a gurgle, and some hard *g* sounds, *ga*, and *g-g-g*, which passed in the eighth week into a roughened *gh*, a sort of scraping, gargling sound, not in the English language.

Our baby had a leaning to throat sounds; but other babies begin with the lip sounds, and some, it is said, with the trilling *l* and *r*. It seems to be only chance what position of the vocal organs is first used; but after once beginning to articulate, the baby seems to pass from sound to sound by slight changes (probably made accidentally in using the old sounds), and so goes through the list with some regularity.

This practice in sounds may be at first quite without will, a mere overflow of energy

into the vocal organs; but it is highly important none the less, for any creature that is
to use human speech must get the speaking
muscles into most delicate training.   Think
what fine and exact difference in muscular
contractions we must make to be able to say
" ball," and be sure that it will not come out
" pall " !

For a week or two now the baby made a
good deal of progress in control of her body.
She strove valiantly every day to keep her
head erect, and made some little advance.
In the bath she began to push with her feet
against the foot of the tub, so hard that her
mother could not keep the little head from
bumping on the other end.   She pulled
downward with her arms when her mother
held them up in wiping her.   These pushing
and pulling movements may have been made
for the pleasure of the feeling, or they may
have been involuntary.   Perhaps they were
accidental movements, passing gradually into
voluntary ones.   In either case, as they de-

veloped, the old irregular movements of legs and arms passed away, as those of the head and face had done before.

One new bit of muscular control was undoubtedly voluntary — a trick of putting out and drawing back the tip of her tongue between her pursed lips. And this was something more than just one new voluntary movement. The important thing was that she was using the movement to *bring together the evidence of two different senses into one perception.*

When something touches against our fingers, we have one sort of feeling in them, and quite another when we pass them over the thing and "feel of it;" and this other, clearer feeling is really a compound one, made up of the touch sensation in the skin and the muscle sensation in the moving fingers. It is called "active touch," and it is a wonderful key to the world around us — so wonderful that with this alone it proved possible to educate Laura Bridgman and

Helen Keller. This active touch the baby
had now developed in tongue and lips; not
yet in the fingers.

The passive sensation of light had already
been blended with muscle sensation in something the same way, by the voluntary movement of turning and focusing the eyes; but
that complete seeing which we might call
"active sight" is a more complex power
than active feeling, and there were other associations yet to be made before it could be
fully built up. And I hope it will not spoil
the interest of the story of the baby's sense
development if I say here that the plot is
going to turn mainly on these two combinations, muscle sense with sight and muscle
sense with touch; and then recombination
of these two with each other — all welded
together by voluntary movements, growing
out of involuntary ones.

All this time the baby had had a daily
source of placid pleasure in listening to
chords on the piano — no longer heavy stac-

cato chords, but flowing ones, in the middle
octaves.   The baby of theory cares for nothing but eating and sleeping; but our
baby, even after she was already fretting
with hunger, would forget all about it for
ten minutes, if one would take her to the
piano.   Hunger, after it grew really strong,
was a sensation that swept all before it; but
on the whole, food was a matter of small
interest compared with the world of light
and touch and sound.

As for sleep, the baby slept, from the first,
in pretty long periods, — six and seven hours
was not uncommon, — and was wide awake
between sleeps.   At such times she would lie
by the half hour, looking peacefully about
her, or gazing into our faces with smiles.
When we nodded, laughed, and talked to
her, her smiles seemed like friendly re-
sponses; but this could have meant nothing,
except that with our demonstrations those
little constellations of high lights and glitters,
our faces, bobbed and twinkled in a more
amusing manner than ever.

At eight weeks old came the final stage
in mastery of the mechanism of vision — the
power of accommodation, or adjusting the
lenses for different distances. It may have
been present even earlier : it is a hard thing
for the observer to know. But the indications are that it really did happen when I
thought, the day the baby was eight weeks
old. She was lying on her mother's knees,
fixing an unusually serious and attentive
gaze on my face, and would not take her
eyes away ; indeed, as her mother turned her
in undressing, she screwed her head around
comically to keep her eyes fixed. At last,
after some fifteen minutes, she turned her
head clear over, and gazed as earnestly at
her mother's face. To see what she would
do, her mother turned her again toward
me, and once more she surveyed me for a
time, and again turned her head and looked
directly at her mother.

What was in the little mind ? Was she
beginning to discriminate and compare, for

the first time setting apart as two separate things the two faces that had bent over her oftenest? Or was she simply using, on the most convenient object, a new power of adjusting her eyes, which filled her with serious interest by the new clearness it gave to what she saw? At all events, she would not have looked from one to the other with such long and attentive regard if she had not been able to focus both faces, at their different distances; so that I felt sure the power of accommodation was really there.

But there was more in the incident than just the advance in vision. Hitherto when the baby had turned her head to look, it had been only at something that she had already a glimpse of, off at the edge of the field of vision. Now she turned to look for something quite out of sight, — something, therefore, that must have been present as an *idea* in the little mind, or she could not have looked for it. And in view of what I have said of the mother's face as the great educational appliance in the early months, it is worth noticing that it was this which gave the baby her first idea, so far as I could detect.

We come a step nearer, too, to true memory, when the baby can keep thus, even for a few minutes, the idea of something formerly seen. It was still mainly habit memory, however. She looked for an accustomed sight in an accustomed place, bringing it to the point of clear vision by an accustomed movement of the neck muscles. There was no evidence till considerably later that she was capable of remembering a single, special experience.

The next day she was singularly bright and sunny, smiling all day at every one. She stopped in the middle of nursing to throw her head back and gaze at the bow at her mother's neck, and would not go on with the comparatively uninteresting business of food till the bow was put out of sight. That night she slept eight hours at a stretch, longer than she had ever done. Was the little brain, perhaps, wearied with the new rush of impressions, which came with the new power of focusing?

The day after she would lie a while unusually silent and sober, looking about her and moving her hands a little; then she would fret to be lifted and held against one's shoulder, where she could hold her head up and look about. She was able now to hold it up a long time by resting it for a few seconds every half minute or so, against my cheek, which I held close to give her the chance. But to-day she was not satisfied with having her head erect: she persistently straightened her back up against the arm that supported her — a new set of muscles thus coming under control of her will. As often as I pressed her down against my shoulder, she would fret, and straighten up again and set to work diligently looking about her.

After this her progress in holding up her head was suddenly rapid, and by the end of the month, four days later, she could balance it for many minutes, with a little wobbling. This uncertainty soon disappeared, and the erect position of the head was accomplished for life.

During these last days of the month the baby was possessed by the most insatiate impulse to be up where she could see. It was hard to think that her fretting and even wailing when forced to lie down could mean only a formless discontent, and not a clear idea of what she wanted. Still, it is not uncommon, when an instinct is thwarted, to feel a dim distress that makes us perfectly wretched without knowing why. As soon as she was held erect, or propped up sitting amid cushions, she was content; but the first time that she was allowed to be up thus most of the day, she slept afterward nine unbroken hours, recuperating, probably, quite as much from the looking and the taking in that the little brain and eyes had been doing as from any muscular fatigue there may have been in the position.

Such is the " mere life of vegetation " the baby lived during the first two months.   No grown person ever experiences such an expansion of life, such a progress from power to power in that length of time.   Nor was our little girl's development anything unusual for a healthy, well-conditioned child, so far as other records give material for comparison.   Preyer's boy was later than she in getting his head balanced, but he arrived at full accommodation (and that is the most important work of the first two months) at almost exactly the same age as she ; and so did Mrs. Hall's boy.   I do not know of any other records that make a clear statement on this point.

VI

PROGRESS TOWARD GRASPING.

THE baby's development, as I have said, consisted now mainly in forming association groups in her mind in two series, which we might call a sight-motor series and a touch-motor series. There had been a leap forward in the sight-motor series when " accommodation " was learned. Now the touch-motor series came to the front, and step by step led on to the great accomplishment of grasping.

First, when we laid the baby's face up against ours, her little tongue was put out to lick the cheek that she felt, warm and smooth, against her lips. This was a more advanced use of active feeling than the mere passing of her tongue over her own lips, for that must have been done accidentally many times before she began to do it on purpose ; and the association between the movement and the feeling had been helped by the double sensation — one feeling in the lips and another in the tongue every time they touched.

This doubling of sensation, which occurs every time one part of the body touches another part, often seemed to wake special attention in the baby, and thus help on a development. Later, it had a great part to play in teaching her the boundaries of her own body, and the difference between the Me and the Not-me. Even now, she must have been somewhat aware of a different feeling when she passed her tongue over her own sensitive lips, and when she passed it over the unresponsive cheek of some one else.

So far, the tongue, not the hand, was her organ of touch. But now the fingers were showing the first faint sign of their future powers — nothing more than a little special sensibility, such as the lips had shown in the first month : we would see the baby holding her finger tips together prettily (when by chance they had collided), as if there were a feeling there that interested her.   Here again there was double sensation.

In these same early days of the third month there was beginning another development that was to end by making the hand the successful rival of lips and tongue for purposes of grasping and feeling.   The baby was trying to get her fists to her mouth.

The movement of the hands toward the head is a common one in the first weeks, by reason of prenatal habit, and thus it had often happened that the little fists, or as much of them as could be accommodated, had blundered into the mouth ; and interesting sensations (double sensations again, in fists and mouth) had been experienced. The baby had at the same time felt in her arms the movement that always went with these interesting sensations, and now she

was trying to repeat it.   Within a week she
had mastered it, and could mumble and suck
her fists at will — a great addition, naturally,
to the comfort of life.

Meanwhile the reflex clasping, which had
always taken place when an object was laid
in the baby's palm, was growing firmer and
longer, and more like conscious holding;
and I noticed that the thumb was now " op-
posed " in clasping — that is, shut down
opposite the fingers, an important element
in the skill of human grasping.   And now,
when the fingers came in contact with convenient things — folds of the towel, for instance — the hands would clasp them mechanically, just as the lips, since the first
month, had laid hold on a breast or cheek
that touched them.

This had an important result.   The little
hand would presently go to the mouth, still
mechanically clasping the fold of towel or
dress, which in consequence was sucked and
mumbled, too.   In this way the baby got

sundry novel sensations, and a chain of associations began to form : she was to learn thus, by and by, that when she felt touch sensations in her fingers, she could get livelier ones in her mouth (and also the pleasant muscular feeling of sucking), by the movements of clasping, and of lifting her arm. But she had not yet learned it : objects (except her own hands) were still carried to her mouth only by accident.

By the twelfth week the baby had found that her thumb was better for sucking purposes than chance segments of fist, and could turn her hand and get the convenient little projection neatly into her mouth. She got hold of it more by diving her head down to it than by lifting the hand to the mouth. Seizing with the mouth, by motions of the head, like a dog, instead of using the hand to wait on the mouth, seemed still her natural way.

But the hands were gaining. In this same twelfth week I saw the little fingertips go fumbling and feeling over our hands and dresses. They, too, had learned active touch, as the tongue had learned it more than a month before.

Just at this time we began to bring the baby to the table — nominally so that no one need stay away from meals to look after her; really for the sake of her jovial company at our sober grown-up board, where she would sit, propped amid cushions in her high chair, gazing and smiling sociably at our faces, crowing and flourishing her arms in joy at the lights and the rattle of dishes, forming the sole topic of conversation to an extent that her bachelor uncle had his private and lonely opinion about. The high chair was one of those that have a wooden tray fastened across the front, and here were placed several handy objects — rattle, and ring, and string of spools. This was by the wisdom of grandma, who saw the approach of the power of grasping. One may often see the little hands fluttering empty, the little brain restless, craving its natural development (for grasping is much more a matter of brain development, through the forming of associations, than of hand development), when there is no wise grandma to see that rattle and ring and spools lie "handy by" a little *before* the baby is ready to use them. To wait till he knows how to grasp before giving him things to practice on is like keeping a boy out of the water till he knows how to swim. Such impeding of the natural activities is responsible for a good deal of the fretting of babies.

It was not three days till I saw the little hands go fumbling across the tray, seeking the objects they had become used to finding there; and when they touched rattle or spool, they laid hold on it. Nor was this the old mechanical clasping: it was voluntary action, and as clumsy as new voluntary action is apt to be, compared to involuntary. The baby did not know how to turn her hand and take up a thing neatly: if she touched it in such fashion that she could shut down her fingers on it somehow or anyhow, she would manage to lift it — stuck between two fingers from behind, once, when the back of her hand had touched it; if not, she would go on fumbling till she did. In two or three days more she was laying hold on things and carrying them to her mouth with plain intention.

Here was a sort of grasping, but it was grasping by feeling only. The baby had yet no idea of an object, which she could locate with the eye and then lay hold on with the hand. She had simply completed the chain of association I spoke of above: she had learned, that is, that after certain groping movements, feelings of touch appeared in her hands; and that then, after movements of clasping and lifting, these feelings reappeared in more lively and pleasing form in her mouth. She never looked at the objects she touched. There is no reason to think they could have been to her anything more than sensations in her own hands and mouth. The sight-motor and touch-motor series had not yet coalesced. But in these last days of the third month both had come to the point where they were ready to begin the fusing process, and give the baby her world of outer objects.

Before I go back to relate what had been going on meanwhile in the sight-motor series, I must stop to speak of some other developments of the month.

Memory, for one thing, had plainly advanced. By the tenth week the baby had shown some doubtful signs of knowing one face from another; and in the twelfth she plainly recognized her grandfather with a smile and joyous cry, as he came in. Her first recognition, therefore (it is worth while to notice), was not of the mother, the source of supplies, but of the face that had offered most entertainment to the dawning mental powers, not only because of the white beard, the spectacles, and the shining bald brow, but because of the boyish abandon with which grandpa played with her, ducking his face down to hers.

A few days later she showed that she knew at least the feeling of her mother's arms. For some weeks no one else had put her to sleep ; and now when sleepy she fretted in other arms, but nestled down contentedly and went to sleep as soon as she felt herself in her mother's.   The association of that especial feeling had become necessary to sleep.

The instinctive language of sign and sound had developed a good deal.   From the first day of the month, the baby's joy in sights began to be expressed more exuberantly, with flying arms and legs, with panting, murmuring, and babbling, smiles and even small chuckles, and sometimes little shouts and crows.   A new look of grief, too, the parallelogram shaped mouth that all babies make in crying, appeared.

In the tenth week she began to turn her head aside in refusal or dislike — a gesture that one may see far down in the animal kingdom. A dog, for instance, uses it very expressively. It comes plainly from the simple effort to turn away from what is unpleasant, and develops later to our shake of the head for " No ; " and when we notice how early the development of control over head and neck is, how much in advance of any use of the hands, we see that it is natural for this to be the oldest of all gestures.

In the last days of the month came two notable evidences of growing will. One was the baby's persistent effort to get the tip of her rattle (it was set on a slender ivory shaft) into her mouth. Sometimes it went in by chance ; sometimes it hit her lip, and in that case she would stretch her mouth to take it in, moving her head rather than the rattle. But if it brought up against her cheek, too far away to be captured by such efforts, after trying a little, she would lower the rattle, and make a fresh start for better luck.

This may seem highly unintelligent action; yet after all, as Professor Morgan says, it is by the method of " trial and error " that most of our acts of skill (and perhaps all such acts of the lower animals) are learned. In trial after trial the baby associated the muscular feeling of the successful movement with the feeling of the rattle tip in her mouth, and repeated these movements more and more correctly, dropping the unsuccessful ones. In just this way the sharpshooter, through repeated trials and misses, learns to deflect his rifle barrel this way and that with an infinite fineness of muscular contractions, which he could never get by reasoning on it.

The other effort of will was in sitting up. During the whole month the baby had insisted on a sitting position, and had wailed as vigorously over being left flat on her back as over being left hungry. She had soon tried to take the matter into her own hands, and made many efforts to lift herself, some-

times by pulling on our fingers when we had
laid them in her hands, sometimes by sheer
strain of the abdominal muscles. She never
succeeded in raising more than her head and
shoulders till the last week of the month :
then she did once lift herself, and in the
following days tried with the utmost zeal to
repeat the success. She would strive and
strain, with a grave and earnest face, her
whole baby soul evidently centred on the
achievement. She would tug at our fingers
till her little face was crimson ; she would
lift her head and shoulders and strain to rise
higher, fall back and try it again, till she
was tired out. The day she was three
months old, she tried twenty-five times,
with scarcely a pause, and even then, though
she was beginning to fret pitifully with dis-
appointment, she did not stop of her own
accord.

Unless she began with a somewhat high
reclining position, or her feet or hips were
held, her little legs would fly up, and she

could not get the leverage to lift her body. For that matter, even with us the legs are lighter than the trunk, and few women can overcome the difference, and lift themselves by sheer strength of the abdominal muscles, without having the feet held : and a baby's legs are so much lighter than ours that it must be for several years a sheer impossibility for him to do it.

However, in the few cases when the baby did manage, by some advantage of position, or by holding to our fingers, to lift herself, she could not balance in the least, and toppled over at once. What with this discouragement, and restraint from her elders, who thought her back by no means strong enough yet for sitting alone, she soon after gave up the effort to raise herself, and waited till she was older.

It was in this same eventful thirteenth week that the baby first looked about, searching for something that was out of sight. A lively young girl with bright

color and a charming pair of dangling eye-
glasses was visiting us, and stood by, laughing and prattling to the baby while she was
bathed. The little one, greatly interested,
turned her head, smiling and crowing, to
watch Miss Charmian's movements, and to
look for her when she was out of sight. In
this, as in the definite efforts to feel the rattle tip in her mouth, and to renew the sensations of sitting up, we see action guided
by an idea of that which is absent, that is
by imagination, to a certain extent at least;
though it is probable that there was still as
much of the mere working of association as
of definite ideas. The memory that the
baby showed when she looked about, searching for an expected sight, instead of simply turning to an accustomed place, is clearly
more than mere habit memory. Yet it was
still not true memory: it was not an idea
coming back to the mind after an interval,
but only a sort of after-shine of the thing,
held in the mind for a few moments after
the thing itself had disappeared.

And now to come back to the sight-motor series : Did the baby still see objects only as blurs of light and shade ? She had the full mechanism of her eyes in working order as soon as accommodation was acquired ; but it is certain that it takes much practice to learn to use that mechanism. It is an old story that people born blind, receiving their sight by surgical operations, have to *learn* to see. Professor Preyer quotes from Dr. Home the case of a twelve year old boy who, nearly a month after the operation, could not tell whether a square card had corners or not by looking at it; and of another seven year old boy who had to learn to recognize triangles and squares (which he knew well by touch) by running his eye along the edges and counting the corners. It must have taken immense practice for us all to learn to flash the eye so quickly over and about an object that we seem to take in its shape with one look. This was the task that lay before the baby now.

How long it took we can only guess. Some observers have taken it for granted that the first recognition of a face showed clear seeing had arrived. But the group of lights and shades is so different in each face that a baby might well learn to know them apart without distinct outlines. We have all seen French paintings in which the eyes, the smile, some high lights on cheek, chin, and nose, and a cloudy suggestion of hair and beard, are all that emerge from the dark canvas, and yet we may see easily for whom the portrait is meant. Our baby had recognized no face yet except her grandfather's, where the beard, spectacles, and shining bald brow made recognition easy without any outline.

But in another direction we get a plainer hint. I have spoken above of the joyous excitement roused in the baby by interesting sights (not only faces now, but also sundry bright things, and dangling, moving things) early in the month. By the middle of the

month her smiles were fewer, and she looked
about her earnestly and soberly ; and in the
last week I noted, without understanding,
the expression of surprise that had come into
her face as she gazed this way and that.
The wide, surprised eyes must have meant
that something new was before them.   Were
things perhaps beginning to separate themselves off to the baby's sight in definitely
bounded spaces ?

I must go on into the record of the next
month for more light on this question : for
the wonder grew day by day, and for weeks
the baby was looking about her silently,
studying her world.   She would inspect the
familiar room carefully for many minutes,
looking fixedly at object after object till the
whole field of vision was reviewed, then she
would turn her head eagerly and examine
another section ; and when she had seen all
she could from one place, she would fret till
she was carried to another, and there begin
anew her inspection of the room in its

changed aspect — always with the look of
surprise and eagerness, eyes wide and brows
raised.

We can only guess what was going on in
the baby mind all this time; but I cannot
resist the thought that I was looking on at
that very process which must have taken
place somewhere about this time — the
learning to see things clear and separate,
by running the eyes over their surfaces and
about their edges.

With this, sight and muscle sense alone,
touch and muscle sense alone, had done all
they could to reveal the world to the baby,
and there lay close before her the further
revelations that were to be made when touch,
sight, and muscle sense could be focused all
together on the objects about her. It was
a wonderful sight to see, as the baby pressed
forward to the new understanding, eager,
amazed, and absorbed.

VII

SHE LEARNS TO GRASP, AND DISCOVERS THE WORLD OF THINGS

THE baby had finished her first quarter year. A few days before, as we have seen, she had looked for a person out of sight; and now, just at the end of the third month, she showed that she could bring together the testimony of sight and hearing, by turning to look in the direction of a sound.

Here seems evidence that by this time (whether she had done so before or not) she " externalized " her impressions more or less : that is, when waves of sound struck on her tympanum, or of light on her retina, she did not simply *feel* the resulting sensation, but threw it back, so to speak, along the line of the wave, and seemed to herself to perceive something outside there, away from her.

For when she looked around, seeking what she did not yet see, expecting sight sensations and hearing sensations to come from the same source, it is impossible to think she did not have a feeling of something really there, outside herself.

Step by step with the sense of outsideness there must have come a sense of insideness, of self, for the two are only opposite sides of one feeling — that is, the feeling of *difference* between oneself and the outer world. We must not suppose that before the baby externalized her impressions she felt everything as happening inside her: she must have just felt things, with no inside or outside about it.

This may seem impossible, but really the sense of insideness and outsideness is not hard to upset, even at our time of life. Dizziness or mental shock will do it. Sometimes on waking from deep sleep we find our sense of a separate bodily self gone, and gather it slowly back. We may almost lose ourselves by lying idly, without thought or care, in some great, continuous sound, like the roar of a cataract, till we do not know which is ourself and which is the outward sound. Mystics and ecstatics have made an art of changing the bodily feelings by fasting and other means, till the usual marks of difference among impressions, by which we externalize some and refer others to our own bodies, are lost; and with them the sense of being in the body, surrounded by an outer world.

Though she externalized sight and sound, it is not likely that the baby at this stage distinguished external and internal in touch impressions, unless about her face. She had not at all learned the bounds of her own body yet. Below her arms, her control of it was almost nothing. She could not turn herself over. She had never passed her hands over her own surface, and knew it only by chance touches. She understood so little her relation even to her hands, which were fairly under control, that when they met by chance, each hand would seize the other, and try to take it to her mouth. She was often aggrieved by the unexpected result when she tried to flourish her arm and go on sucking her thumb at the same time, and could not imagine what had suddenly snatched the cherished thumb away. Her feeling of herself must have been very different from ours : more like that of a conventional cherub, all but her head dissolved away into oneness with the outside world.

Did she, then, seeing the vision of the world, see it as a world of *things* — solid objects, visible and tangible ? Probably not. Her whole behavior showed that she had never blended the feel of a thing and the look of a thing into the perception of the thing itself. If her body was touched anywhere, she never looked toward the place to see what touched her. When she groped on her tray, she seemed to be merely repeating motions that had formerly brought sensations, not seeking for things that she supposed were there; she never looked for them, nor even looked at them as she held them; she seemed to have no suspicion that the feeling in her hand was due to a visible object there.

Nor could she well have had any idea of an object, even as one may get it from touch alone, without sight; for she did not feel over the things she held — she was conscious only of the part that touched her. If she laid hold of her rattle one day by one part, and another day by another, she could not have known it was the same object, except as she learned a little about it in fumbling for a better hold. In short, the things she touched and held can hardly have been to her definite objects, but only disjointed touch and weight sensations.

With no more material than this, children born blind do build up in time the idea of a world of things; but seeing children have a much quicker and completer way.

Just at the end of the third month the baby had once gazed at her rattle as she held it in her hand; but it was not till the second week of the fourth month that she seemed really to learn that when she felt the familiar touch in her hand, she could see something by looking. Then her eyes began to rest on things while she picked them up; but in a blank and passive way — the eyes looking on like outsiders, while the awkward little hands fumbled just as they would have done in the dark. The baby seemed to have no idea that what she saw was the same thing as what she felt.

There was about a fortnight of this. Then, on one great day, when three weeks of the month had passed, the baby looked at her mother's hand, held up before her, and made fumbling motions toward it, keeping her eyes on it, till her hand struck it; then took hold of it. She had formed an association between the sight of an object and the groping movement of her hand toward it.

It was not till the last week of the month that she put out her hand directly to the thing she wanted, instead of clawing vaguely toward it; and even then it was doubtfully done. Still, it was real grasping, by guidance of the eye. She was coming to realize that what she saw was one with what she could feel; that there were *things*, which could be reached for and got hold of. That is, the sight-motor series and the touch-motor series were coalescing at last, and giving the baby a world of objects. She had an immensity to learn as to their form, weight, distance, and all that; but she had the key now for learning it.

The discovery of the new quality of tangibility in the visible world must have been gradual, however, and her new power of grasping hardly more at first than a blind use of association. In the next fortnight she grasped doubtfully, depending only partly on sight for guidance. She would put out her hand uncertainly, with fingers

spread, not ready to grasp, and it was only
when they touched the object that her movement became confident. Sometimes both little hands were brought cautiously down on
either side of the thing she wished to get
hold of.

In this fortnight she grasped better with
the mouth than with the hands, and was
more disposed to use it. She brought her
mouth to the nipple easily by sight. She
dived at me with her head to get the loose
folds of my bodice into her mouth. In our
arms, she would attack our faces with a sudden dive of her head and a funny doubling
up movement of her body, and would mouth
them over with satisfaction. One day, as
she lay on her back, a rubber ring fell out
of her mouth, and lay encircling her nose,
resting on its bridge and on the upper lip;
she made many efforts to reach it with her
lips, stretching her mouth open ridiculously,
but had no idea of using the little hands,
which were fluttering wildly in helpless sympathy.

During this early period of grasping, the baby was far from appreciating what a world of delight had opened to her. Her great interest all the fourth month and on into the fifth was in the use of her eyes, in those eager surveys of things that I have spoken of; and absorbed in this, she had unconsciously and almost mechanically gathered together the associations of sight and feeling and muscle sense, till grasping had come about, merely as a more efficient way of getting things into the mouth.

Professor Preyer and most other observers have tried to account for this persistent drift of everything to the baby's mouth by the theory of taste association: the baby's most agreeable experience has been that of tasting milk, and so he connects all pleasure with the idea of getting things to his mouth. This seems to me quite untenable. An association between taste and the feeling of something in the mouth would not be formed unless the two occurred together quite regu-

larly; and what with the washing out of a
baby's mouth each time he is nursed, and
the frequent stumbling in of his hands, and
later the deliberate sucking of fists, he finds
tasteless objects there oftener than milk.
Again, it is not the movement of the hands
up to the mouth that would become associated with food, but rather the feeling of
being laid at the breast (which our baby
did in fact associate early with food, as I
have related).   And in the third place, there
is not the least evidence that taste is the
most agreeable experience of young babies;
on the contrary, the tests go to show that
they have a low taste sensibility.

The craving of hunger, of course, is an
intense feeling in babies, and its satisfaction (rather than taste pleasure) is greatly
enjoyed; but except just at the hungry moment, they pay far more attention to looking, and hearing, and feeling than to eating.
Our baby, after the first edge of hunger was
off, was always ready to desert the breast to

look at something interesting. She would nurse a little, then throw herself back on her mother's arm to smile up into her face. She cried quite as hard over being obliged to lie down, where she could not look around her, as over being hungry ; and getting her meal caused no such marked signs of pleasure as light and motion, the bath, and the free use of her own powers.

Some babies are hungrier than ours was, and some are like her; but I think close observation would show all alike more taken up with their higher powers than with food. And as all alike put everything into their mouths when they first learn to grasp, we must find some other reason for the act than food association.

If we regard it as an exercise of the sense of touch, in what is at the time the main touch organ, we have an activity closely parallel with the constant interest in the use of sight in the early months. Observers have been misled by failing to realize that the

mouth, not the hand, is the primitive touch
organ. The baby behaves with the things
in his mouth as if he was interested in feeling them, not in eating them. He does not
try to swallow them (though he may be de-
pended on to do it without trying, if they
are small), but licks, sucks, mumbles them
about, and in every way gets the utmost
touch sensation out of them. Preyer saw a
look of pleasure caused by sucking a pencil,
before the baby had ever tasted food, when
he could not have had the least taste association with the feeling. There is plenty of
evidence that the act of sucking (the muscular sensation as well as that of touch) is in
itself highly agreeable to babies.

I have spoken of the great and active interest, at this time, in studying the visible
world. By the end of the fourth month the
baby had certainly learned the look of many
things, and was well aware when it was in
any way changed. In a strange room she
would renew the eager and surprised staring

about which had nearly ceased in familiar rooms ; and if one of us appeared in a bonnet she would look with curiosity and interest at our changed aspect. She doubtless knew us all apart by this time, though she gave no clear evidence of it, except in the case of grandpa, whom she often greeted with cries of joy and flying hands.

From the middle of the fourth month she followed us constantly with her eyes as we moved about. Her eyes were thus drawn to greater distances, and her range of vision increased ; before this she had hardly noticed anything across the room. In the latter part of the month she looked with especial curiosity at people's faces on the other side of the room, and I guessed that it was because they looked so much smaller to her — as they would to us if we had not learned to allow for the distance. A face fifteen feet away can be completely hidden by a fifty cent piece held out at arm's length ; our friends shrink to small dolls in our eyes every time

they cross the room, but we bring them up
to their real size by trained imagination.
The baby, who had not yet the trained imagination, must have seen strange shrink-
ings and swellings as people moved from her
or toward her, and as she was carried about
the room.

She saw a complete change of appearance,
too, each time any one turned around, and
each time she was carried from one side to
another of a person, or of a piece of furniture. We have become so used to this that
we do not notice it; but to the baby each
side of an object must have looked like an
entirely new thing. I think it was some
time before she learned to associate together
the different sides and the different sizes of
each object — all the aspects one chair could
take, for instance, gathering into one group
in her mind, and all the aspects a table or
a person could take, into another; but she
was learning. It was an enormous piece of
work for the baby brain, but babies are not
lazy, and she enjoyed it.

The changes that people went through, as they moved about, were much more complicated than those of the furniture; but that only made them the more interesting. No wonder that as soon as the baby knew she could touch and feel what she saw, it was our faces she dived for with especial zeal, to explore their surfaces with her mouth; and a fortunate thing it is for the baby's progress in knowledge that mothers do not mind having great and moist liberties taken with their faces. Our baby learned, too, at this time, with the connivance of her grandfather, and afterward her father, to fix her fingers in their beards and tug. This was doubtless educational, and it brought still another interest into the number that gathered about the faces of her fellow beings: but it led to trouble later, as her hands grew quicker and stronger in clutching.

She was a joyous and sociable little being in those days, and while her serious business was looking about and studying out the visi-

ble world, or exploring with her mouth the
feeling of things, her delight was as always
in people's faces and attentions. She had become charmingly responsive, and answered to
nods and prattle and cuddling with the gay-
est of smiles and crows, and lively flourishing of arms and legs. From early in the
month she acquired an ecstatic little chuckle,
and once or twice even broke into a genuine
laugh when she was played with a little more
boisterously than usual.

For by this time, and more and more every
week, she began to like a frolic, and when
she was tossed, rolled over, or slid down
one's knee, she crowed and beamed and
chuckled in high delight. She was such a
tiny baby for rough play that we tumbled
her about most gingerly, but she seemed
ready for anything herself. She was a baby
singularly free from fear or nervous excita-
bility, showing already quite clearly the
temperament she has carried through her
later childhood.

She was also physically strong, and once or twice in the fourth month sat quite alone on some one's lap. I do not count this real sitting alone, however, for the lap gives under the baby's weight, and steadies her a little : one should not record sitting alone till the baby has balanced successfully on a hard level, the floor or table. But as far as strength of back was concerned, our baby was now evidently ready to sit alone.

At this stage the babies of grandpa's line have always been seated on the floor in a horse-collar, as befitted farm babies ; and this latest one went into the collar at four months old, like the rest of us in our day, and spent much of her fifth month sitting there, sucking or brandishing her rattle, and looking happily about her. It is really a comfortable seat for a baby not yet quite ready to sit alone. When the collar is not brand new, one will of course scrub and disinfect it ; and it is the better in any case for a blanket or thick shawl thrown over it.

Also of course, one will never set a baby on the floor without seeing that all possible drafts, under doors or about loose window casings, are shut off with shawls and screens. Otherwise, there may be pneumonia to fight.

I have just spoken of the baby's boldness. She showed fear now and then, however. About the middle of the fourth month she cried while a caller was present, dressed in black, with a large hat. Ten days later she was quite upset when her father leaned over suddenly, bringing his face into view from one side. Here were the first eye fears, considerably later than ear fears.

A still more advanced form of fear appeared two days later. The baby had waked and cried alone in the dark for some minutes, and when she was at last taken up, she had evidently become frightened, and was not easily reassured; she kept leaning toward her mother, and uttering troubled cries, and as it was some minutes before her mother took her, she grew more and more disturbed, and finally broke into a wail, and was soothed with difficulty, and all the evening she was anxious and easily upset. The next night, waking alone at the same hour, she began again to cry with the note of fright.

Here was not yet fear in the sense of definite expectation of harm. It was still purely instinctive, a sort of vague panic, from a sense of unfamiliarity. The darkness no doubt contributed to this unfamiliarity, but I do not think there was yet anything that could be called fear of the dark. It is doubtless, however, in large part from such experiences that fear of the dark is born ; each one leaves its trace in the nervous system, and associations of terror with darkness and solitude are quickly formed. In these days of leaving babies to wail themselves to sleep for the good of their souls, and the convenience of mamma's going out evenings, innumerable such associations. must be bred — and again the schoolbooks take the blame when in later days the child proves nervous and excitable.

During the latter part of the fourth month, the baby was greatly interested in making sounds, and the one that most delighted her was a sort of harsh cawing or croaking, made deep in the throat, on the vowel $\hat{a}$. She would lie and utter this sound at intervals, by the half hour, with deep satisfaction. But when she had not been making it for some hours, she was apt to forget just how, and to get it too high or low in the throat, producing an extraordinary collection of squeaks and grunts. She usually hit it at last; but after repeated losings, it became quite dissolved away among the many new ones it had apparently given rise to.

Later, she took much pains over some imperfect lip sounds; she would lie looking earnestly at me, draw her breath, gather her lips into shape, and finally explode the sound with a great expenditure of breath.

She made her little sounds often with an air of friendly response when we prattled to her, giving back murmurs, croaks, and gur-

gles for words. From the latter part of the
fourth month, if we imitated to her some of
these sounds, she seemed to imitate them
back. Preyer, who records the same thing
of his boy at the same age, thinks it marks
a most important epoch, the beginning of
action guided by ideas ; but Baldwin, who
considers the beginning of imitation even
more important than Preyer does, thinks it
cannot be so early, and that the repeating
of the sounds must be mere coincidence.

This is likely enough, for a baby is always
repeating his pet sounds, and it is not safe
to conclude that he means to imitate us, even
if he does chance to give back the same
sound after us several times. But as to action guided by ideas, we scarcely need wait
for the first imitation to see that. It appears
in a simple form when the baby first looks
for an object out of sight. This our baby
had done weeks before, and by this time
many of her actions seemed to be of ideo-
motor type. The effort to recall her croak

was an instance. In the early weeks of the fifth month, she would seem to think suddenly of one of her little sounds, and dash at it, bringing it out with a comical doubling up of her body. In the same way she would have the happy thought, " Fingers in mouth ! " and up they would come with a jerk, her head diving forward to meet them.

In the nineteenth week, she seemed to act once from something like a definite memory. Her grandfather entered the room while she was in her bath, and her usual joyous up and down movement of arms at sight of him produced a novel and fascinating splashing. Next day the baby splashed without suggestion, and again the next, looking up to my face and smiling; and after that no one could teach her anything about splashing. Yet even this was probably not really memory, but an association formed by a single vivid occurrence.

During these weeks a note of real desire, unheard before, appeared in her voice. Her face had at times, when she saw something new, or when she gazed at us while we talked to her, an expression of inquiry and effort to comprehend, with lips drawn in and brow tense.   No one could watch her and not see the beginnings of some sort of mental life.

VIII

THE ERA OF HANDLING THINGS

SHE sprang into this era suddenly, within four days. It was not infrequently thus, and perhaps more and more as the little brain grew complex. Some power that had been slowly developing would leap up into completion, unlocking a dozen other doors of mental life. To put it physiologically, some one new connection established between brain cells would bring a whole network of others into coöperation — the more easily as ancestral nerve paths seemed often to open up at a touch.

When the baby had passed ten days of her fifth month, she was still grasping half mechanically. On the eleventh day, lying on her back, she held her rattle above her and looked at it carefully. Her attention had turned to the things that she grasped. She had come before to the perception of a world of objects, but apparently only now to the realization of it. And thereupon, that very day, I saw that she was no longer using eyes and hands merely as means of getting mouth sensations; she was holding objects, looking at them, and pulling them about, for some moments, before they went to her mouth.

The pleasure of this handling seemed to be in the free movement of the objects (seen and felt at the same time), not especially in the touch sensations. When this new pleasure was exhausted, things went to the mouth as before for the enjoyment of touch. It was long before the fingers rivaled the lips in pure æsthetic touch enjoyment; perhaps they never do, else the dandy would finger his cane knob, instead of mouthing it, girls would smooth rose-leaves across their finger tips, not their lips, and a kiss would have no higher rank than a hand clasp. But for grasping purposes the supremacy now passed promptly over to the hands, and from this week the habit of grasping with the mouth by head movements declined and disappeared.

In a few hours the baby was reaching for everything near her, and in three days more her desire to lay hold on things was the dominant motive of her life. Her grasping was still oftener with both hands than one, and was somewhat slow, but always accurate. Some babies learn to grasp more suddenly than she did, and often miss their aim; but with her cautious method of bringing down her hands toward an object from either side, penning it in between, she could hardly make errors. The thing once corralled, she would pull it around, perhaps a minute, then put it to her mouth.

It is an epoch of tremendous importance when the baby first, with real attention, brings sight and touch and muscle feeling to bear together on an object. " In a very

deep sense," says John Fiske, "all human
science is but the increment of the power of
the eye, and all human art is the increment
of the power of the hand.   Vision and ma-
nipulation — these in their countless indirect
and transfigured forms are the two coöperat-
ing factors in all intellectual progress."
And the first great result of this coöperation
is the completion of vision itself.   It cannot
be doubted that it is mainly by studying
objects with eye and hand together that we
get our ability to see solid form.   A colt
grasping his ear of corn with his teeth, even
a puppy licking and turning his bone all
over, or a kitten tapping a spool to and fro
and hugging it in her paws, without losing
sight of it — none of these can bring the
united powers of three senses to bear on an
object so perfectly as a monkey or human
baby can, holding it in the most convenient
positions, turning it this way and that, seeing every part, feeling it with finger tips
and mouth ; and it is doubtful if the quad-

rupeds ever attain to as clear a sense of form as we do.

In these first days of the passion for grasping at things, the baby reached for flat figures as readily as for solid objects; but (to look ahead a little) she learned to discriminate with surprising ease, and after the first week I have only three or four notes of her trying to pick up such things as pictures on a page, roses on a quilt, shadows in the sun. Yet I do not think this was because she gained quickly any such sense of the difference between plane and solid form as we have, but rather that she learned quickly to associate a certain look about an object with the experience of being able to get hold of it.

The reason that I think so is that even weeks later, when she was six months old, she showed signs of having no real ability to judge form by the eye. At that age she turned a round cracker round and round at her lips, trying to find the corner to bite, as

she was used to doing with square ones.
And the only time she was ever taken in by
a flat figure afterward was when (at nine
months old) she tried a long time to capture
the swaying shadow of a rope end on the
deck of a yacht; things that moved could
always be taken hold of in her experience,
and she went solely by experience, not by
any general ideas of form.

But such general ideas really require a
good deal of development of reason — so
much that it is likely the lower animals never
rise to them.   We must think of the baby's
seeing, therefore, as rounding out but slowly
to full equality with ours in such matters as
estimates of form, distance, and size, where
much experience and some reason are required.

To go back to those swift four days in
which the baby came into realization of her
power of using hands and eyes together, —
they had been preceded by a marked advance
in the use of eyes alone (or jointly with the

sense of motion in being carried about) to get the relations of things about her more clearly arranged in her mind. The day before the baby held up her rattle to look at, she had declined to go to sleep in her mother's arms, and kept lifting her head to look at me, till I crossed the room and put myself out of sight. Presently she lifted her head again, turned round, and searched persistently the quarter of the room toward which she had seen me disappear. She had gained much in sense of direction and in association of ideas when she could look along the line in which I had been seen to move moments before, expecting to see me somewhere there.

Later, the same day, she sat in my lap, watching with an intent and puzzled face the back and side of her grandmother's head. Grandma turned from her knitting and chirruped to her, and the little one's jaw dropped and her eyebrows went up with an expression of blank surprise. Presently I began to swing her on my foot, and at every pause in the swinging she would sit gazing at the puzzling head till grandma turned, and nodded or chirruped to her; then she would turn away satisfied and want more swinging.

Here we seem to get a glimpse of the process I have spoken of, by which the baby gradually associates together the front and rear and side aspects of a person or thing, till at last they coalesce together in his mind as all one object. At first amazed to see the coil of silver hair and the curve of cheek turn suddenly into grandma's front face, the baby watched for the repetition of the miracle till it came to seem natural, and the two aspects were firmly knit together in her mind.

She began, too, to watch people's motions carefully for long spaces of time — all through the process of setting the table, for instance — with a serious little face, and an attention so absorbed that it was hardly possible to divert her if one tried (which one ought not to do, for power of attention is a precious attainment, and people have no business to meddle with its growth for their own amusement).   When her mother's dark-eyed sister had a little reception in consequence of having married the minister, baby was in the thick of it, watching first the preparations, and then the comings and goings of people, with the closest attention and the deepest enjoyment, cheerfully willing to have her meals postponed, her nap broken, anything, if the fun would only go on.

There was a decided advance, too, in her acquaintance with her own body.   Sitting as usual in her horse-collar, she was bending herself back over it, a thing that she had done before; but to-day she kept it up so persistently, and bent herself back with such exertion, that at last the back of her head touched the floor.   She righted herself with an expression of great surprise.   Evidently she had been experimenting in new muscular sensations only, and (as happens to all experimenters sometimes) had got an extra result that she did not bargain for and did not understand. She bent back again, with her head screwed around to see what had given her the touch. In this position, she did not reach the floor. She sat up again, looked at me with a perplexed face, and tried it over, a full dozen times, till her mother picked her up to stop it, on the ground that the baby was more valuable than the experiment, and that she would break her little back. For days, however, the baby returned to the investigation, doubling herself back over the arm of any one who held her till her head hung straight down, or over the horse-collar till it rested on the floor.

We may perhaps fairly guess that in this incident she had for the first time discovered the back of her head as a part of herself, and any of us might well be surprised to find himself extending off behind into space that way, if he had never known about it before. The baby had of course felt daily and hourly touches on the back of her head, from pillow and floor and lap, from cap and hair brush ;

but all her previous behavior, and her surprise
now, indicate that this was the first time she
had externalized these touches — which implies also the first time she had felt *herself*
as receiving them.

One of the first things she did when she
began grasping zealously was to seize her
own toes, and she bent her foot forward on
the ankle to bring it better in reach. This
may have been a purely instinctive coöperat-
ing act at first, but it helped on the control
of feet and legs, and the recognition of them
as parts of herself — the more as they were
now for some time favorite playthings every
time the baby was undressed.

Another significant movement the next
day, also brought about by the advance in
grasping, was the first attempt to scramble
forward as she lay on her stomach, to get
hold of something — a futile effort, but the
forerunner of creeping.

These days of rapid unfolding were joyous days. The baby laughed aloud more

than ever before, and her daily frolics were as necessary to her as her meals, and were fretted for as persistently if she did not get them. The door of communion with fellow beings, too, was trembling on its hinges, ready to come ajar. The little thing began to look up into our faces as if for sympathy in pleasure or perplexity, as I have mentioned in the case of her surprise at discovering the back of her head; she did it laughing when she splashed in the bath, and with smiles of satisfaction when she listened to the piano. When her mother held out her arms to take her, she learned to put forward her little hands in response; and on the same day she took up the instinctive gesture of stretching out her arms toward an object in desire — always, I suspect (records are wanting), the next gesture after turning away the head. Neither of these reaching gestures was as yet used intentionally to convey ideas, but both entered later into genuine sign language. Both seem to grow naturally out of grasping movements.

In the baby's absorption in grasping, most
of her little sounds were abandoned ; but she
clung to a favorite long gurgle, and used it
with an air of amiable response when people
talked or nodded to her, often kicking her
legs in the air or flinging up her arms, by
way of emphasis.   Sometimes she would look
earnestly into your face and address you with
the gurgle in all seriousness.   Sometimes it
would seem to occur to her suddenly, and
she would burst out with it, with an impulsive movement of body and limbs.

In a few days she had become a different
baby, with a new world of interests, and a
wonderfully more varied and vivid life.   After this, she went on smoothly to the end of
the fifth month (and for that matter, through
the sixth), absorbed in looking, feeling, and
handling, reaching this way and that to lay
hold of everything she saw, and improving
steadily in skill.   A small steel bell given
her in the twenty-first week was at first
pulled and shoved about on the table, picked

up with two fingers or more as might chance, and put into her mouth by any part that came handiest; but in three or four days it was taken up properly and rung.   More and more all the time she found something to do with things besides putting them in her mouth.

She liked hard, bright, and rattling things best to handle, and preferred metal or bone to rubber.   One can hardly think of a thing less useful to a baby educationally at this stage than soft, colored worsted balls; he needs something that he can feel, hard and definite, in his hand; something with distinctly unlike sides that he can see as he pulls and shakes it about; he loves glitter, but cares little for color, perhaps does not yet see it; and any dyes and worsted shreds that can come off in wet little mouths are conclusive against such a toy.

On the other hand, bright metal objects are apt in the course of their gyrations to deal bad thumps to little heads and noses;

so one must compromise on rubber — uninteresting, but safe — and on such bone, metal (perhaps aluminum), and unpainted wooden toys as can be trusted to give only very mild thumps, such as a baby had better take now and then rather than be deprived of all really interesting toys.

This is one of the many dilemmas in which the baby is lucky who has a grandma, or whose mamma can spare time to associate with him a great deal; for no end of things can be trusted in the little hands, that ache for everything in sight, if only vigilant fingers hover close, ready to ward gently off any dangerous movement. Sitting in one's lap at the table, too, the baby may push and pull at many things not safe for him to lift; or he may be allowed to handle something safely tethered with a string. Certainly the wider liberty of holding and handling he can by any device be allowed, the better; the instinct is very strong, and wholly healthy, and the thwarting of normal instincts is not good for any one's nerves or mind.

In sight, important changes were no longer
to be looked for : except possibly in the matter of color sense, the baby's seeing had now
passed through all the stages of development,
and needed only practice and mental growth
to become as perfect as it would ever be.
She was evidently still at work somewhat,
especially in new places, in reducing confused
appearances to order ; but so much of this
work was already done that more and more
she could sit and enjoy the varied spectacle.
More than once she spent half an hour gazing thus out of the window with quiet pleasure.

There were for the first time signs that
she could distinguish between the sounds of
voices. She looked and listened one day in
the middle of the month, as if she noticed
something unusual, when I was hoarse with
a cold. Late in the month, as I read to her
mother while she nursed the baby, singing
softly to her (a frequent custom), the baby
suddenly raised her head and looked curi-

ously at me, evidently for the first time distinguishing the two voices as separate sounds.

Her mother and grandmother had been saying to her a great deal, " Papa!" hoping to hasten her understanding of the word. This same day she imitated the motion of the lips, and seemed to find the feeling very funny, for she laughed, and laughed whenever she heard the sound explosively uttered during the next fortnight; she stopped in the midst of crying to laugh at it. Her amusement had not the faintest connection with the meaning of the word; indeed, she chuckled aloud with even more gayety when I ejaculated " poo-poo!" or " boo-boo!" instead. It was something in the explosive labial sound that struck her as comical.

In this beginning of discrimination in articulate sounds, we see the root of the later understanding of speech. But it was by another road that the baby now began to move toward human communication: by the way, that is, of signs and inarticulate cries.

One day when she was four and a half months old, she raised a strange little clamor on catching sight of her grandfather, as if on purpose to call his attention, and was satisfied when she got it; she began to hold out her arms of her own accord, instead of merely to meet ours, held out to her; and in the very last days of the fifth month she made a sound of request when she wished to be taken, a whimpering, coaxing sound, leaning and looking toward her mother, instead of the mere fretting sounds of desire, addressed to nobody, which she had made for weeks.

When I have spoken before of the baby's "addressing" her little noises to us, I have not meant that there was really anything of language in them. Some expression of interest in our presence, some sort of social feeling, there must have been, but no more than in her kicking up her feet or chuckling at our attentions. These first asking sounds and motions, on the contrary, were beginnings of real language — not yet of human

language, but of such as the baby shares
with all the beasts and birds.

A sort of intelligence shared with the
beasts and birds, too, appeared in these same
closing days of the fifth month — what may
be called " adaptive intelligence," the use of
means to an end — in the patient devices by
which the baby manœuvred her toe into her
mouth; but this was a sort of anticipation
of a development that belonged really to the
next month, and so I shall leave the account
of it to the next.

The increasing ownership of her body that
this toe feat showed was evident in several
other ways.   The baby's sitting up grew im-
perceptibly firmer and more independent of
support: at nineteen weeks old, she was sitting alone in our laps a quarter of a minute
at a time; four days later, a minute at a
time, provided she did nothing to upset herself, such as flourishing her arms, or reaching after things; two days later yet, she
balanced successfully for a few seconds on

the table — and this was real sitting alone at last, for on the table there could be no least support from the yielding of the surface under her.   All babies can sit alone earlier on the lap or a cushion than on a perfectly flat, hard surface.

At just about nineteen weeks old, too, the baby began to roll over to her side when she was laid on her back on the floor, and to squirm and bend around into a variety of positions, instead of lying where she was put.

The period was coming to an end in which the main activity of development was in the senses, and in coming through the coöperation of the senses to a bodily consciousness of herself in a world of objects, of distances, and directions.   Now the baby had to learn to use that body, and explore that world. But before this second great period of activity fully began, there was a transition month, a month of vigorous practice in the powers already gained, and of gathering forces for the new developments.

IX

THE DAWN OF INTELLIGENCE

THE sixth month, though it lay between two great development periods, — that of learning to use the senses, and that of learning to carry the body, — was not in itself a period of suspended development.   It is true that its progress, being more purely mental, could not be so continuously traced as that which came before and after, but rather cropped up to the surface every now and then in a more or less broken way; still, no doubt, it really went on in the same gradual method, one thread and another knitting together into the fabric of new powers.

It was to this month, as I said in closing the last chapter, that the beginnings of adaptive intelligence belonged; and this alone marks it a great epoch.

There is a great deal of discussion about the use of the words "intelligence," "reason," "instinct," "judgment," "inference," and the like: what these faculties and acts really are, how they come about, where the line is to be drawn between their manifestations (in the minds of animals and of man, for instance), and many other problems. But I think that all agree upon recognizing two types of action that come under the discussion: one, that which shows merely the ability to adapt means to ends, to use one's own wit in novel circumstances; the other, that which rests on the higher, abstract reasoning power, such as is hardly possible without carrying on a train of thought in words. Whether these two types are to be called intelligence and reason, as Professor Lloyd Morgan calls them, or whether both come under the head of reason, lower and higher, we need not trouble to decide. If we call them adaptive intelligence and higher or abstract reason, we are safe enough.

Even if it be true that any glimmer of the higher reason penetrates back into the grades of life below the attainment of speech, it must be only into those just below, and is not to be looked for in our baby for a long time yet. But the mere practical intelligence that I am now speaking of seems to appear in babies close on the completion of a fair mastery of their senses, about the middle of the first year, and it goes pretty far down in the animal kingdom. Darwin thought the lowest example of it he knew was in the crab, who would remove shells that were thrown near the mouth of his burrow, apparently realizing that they might fall in.

Recent psychologists have shown strong reason for thinking that such acts as this are at bottom only the same old hit and miss trick that we have seen from the first, of repeating lucky movements; only in a higher stage, as the associations that guide the movements become more delicate and complicated, and memory and imagination enter in. However this may be as a matter of theoretic analysis, there is in practice a clear test of difference between the unintelligent earlier type of actions and those that all agree in calling intelligent : I have indicated it above, in saying that in intelligent action one's own wit must be used " in novel circumstances." The case must be such that one cannot fall back on race instinct nor on his own previous habit.

Our baby, for instance, first used her intelligence to steer her toe into her mouth, and the way she did it, compared with the way she slowly settled on the proper movements for getting her rattle into her mouth, shows clearly the practical difference between unintelligent and intelligent action, even if both are at bottom made of the same psychological stuff.

It was just before the sixth month began that the baby accomplished this feat, but it belongs with the developments of that month. She was already fond of playing with her

toes; and sitting unclad that evening in her
mother's lap, she first tried to pull them
straight to her mouth.   This was, of course,
the mere repetition of a frequent movement,
learned by simple association.   But when it
failed — for the toes would kick away, just
as her arms used to do, carrying the thumb
from her lips — the little one put her mind
on corralling them.   She took them in one
hand, clasped the other hand about her in-
step, and so brought the foot safely up.
Still it escaped, and at last she clasped ankle
and heel firmly, one with each hand, and
after several attempts brought the elusive toe
triumphantly into her mouth.   It is true that
by looking up to us for sympathy in her success, and relaxing attention, she promptly lost
it once more; but she recaptured it, and from
this time on, for weeks, had immense satisfaction in it every time she was undressed.

There may have been a certain element
of instinct in this — getting the toe to the
mouth is so persistent a habit with babies

that it seems as if there must be some inheritance about it; but inheritance could hardly have given the special devices for managing the insubordinate foot; there was clearly some use of individual intelligence. All through the process of learning to manage the body, the baby showed instinct and intelligence most intricately mingled; and, indeed, we do so ourselves our lives long.

Of all a baby's doings this toe business is the one that people find it most impossible to regard with scientific seriousness. But its indirect usefulness is considerable. The cooperation of different parts of the body that it teaches is remarkable; and it must have great influence in extending the sense of self to the legs and feet, where it has hitherto seemed but weakly developed. This is important in getting the body ready for standing and walking.

The baby now showed intelligence in her actions in several little ways, such as tugging with impatient cries at her mother's dress when she wanted her dinner, and leaning over to pluck at the carriage blanket, under which her mother had laid some flowers to keep them from her. She slipped a long-handled spoon farther down in her hand to get the end of the handle into her mouth (almost exactly the same act as the one that Darwin thought first showed " a sort of practical reflection " in his child at about the same age : the boy slipped his hand down his father's finger, in order to get the finger tip into his mouth). In the second week of the month she began to watch things as they fell, and then to throw them down purposely, to watch them falling.

I have already mentioned certain doubtful imitations in the fourth month, and a clearer one in the fifth. Now the baby began to imitate unmistakably. Her uncle had a fashion of slapping his hand down on the table by way of a salutation to her, and one day (when she had passed a week of her sixth month) she slapped down her little hand in return. The next day as soon as her uncle came in, she began to slap her hand down, watching him, delighted to repeat the movement back and forth, as long as he would keep it up. She would imitate me also when I did it; and in the course of the month several other little imitations occurred.

I have already spoken of the great importance psychologists attach to imitation. Professor Baldwin makes it the great principle of development in child and race — all evolution one long history of its workings; but he uses the word in a far wider sense than the ordinary one, tracing " imitation " from the mechanical repetition of life-preserving motions by the lowest living things, up to the spiritual effort of men and women to live up to their own highest ideals. Even using the word in its ordinary sense, we know what a potent force in the little one's education imitation is. The age, however, at which it is most efficient is considerably later than the sixth month, and it did not count for much yet with our baby.

Her sounds had been more various and expressive from the first days of the month. She had taken up a curious puppy-like whine of desire or complaint, and a funny little ecstatic sniffing and catching her breath, to express some shades of delight; and she had also begun to pour out long, varied successions of babbling sounds, which expressed content, interest, or complaint very clearly. She would "talk to" any interesting object (a hedge in gorgeous bloom, for instance) with this expressive babble, sometimes holding out her arms to it at the same time. But now, in the second week of the month, the day after the first decisive imitation, a surprising advance beyond these means of communication took place.

I must explain that the wise grandma, who believed in encouraging babies to creep, as the best possible preparation for standing and walking, had begun to set the little one on her hands and knees on the big dining-table, putting a hand against her feet as a brace in case she should be moved to struggle forward. The baby had a habit of pushing with her feet when she felt anything against her soles; and pushing thus, thrust herself forward; and as the table-cover slid with her movement, she would half slide with it, half shove herself, across the table, grunting with exertion, and highly pleased.

On the day in question I was sitting with her by this table, and she pulled at the table-cover, as she was wont to pull and handle anything she could reach. Suddenly she threw herself back on my arm, and looked earnestly in my face; sat up and pulled at the cover again, then threw herself back and looked at me again.

"What does she want?" I said, surprised, and hardly able to think that the little thing could really be trying to say something to me. But grandma interpreted easily, and when I put the baby on the table accordingly, to make her sliding sprawl across the surface, she was satisfied.

This remarkable advance in sign language comes well under our definition of intelligent action : it was not a stereotyped sign, already fixed in her mind in association with a certain wish, like holding out her arms to be taken, but a device of her own, to meet the special occasion.

Her increased power of communication was not the only way in which her mind showed itself more wide awake to other people. A rather uncomfortable phase of this development was timidity. In the first week of the month, she was frightened by some one who came in suddenly between her and her mother, in a strange house, and spoke abruptly, in a deep, unfamiliar voice ; and after that she often cried or became uneasy when strange men took her, or came near her, especially if they were abrupt. She drew distinct lines, according to some principle of her own, and certain people were affably accepted at once, while others, no more terrific that we could see, made the little lip quiver every time they came near.   This timidity toward people was not at all deeply fixed in her temperament, and though it lasted all this month, it was never very marked afterward.

Some indications of the dawn of affection also appeared now.   The baby's desire to touch our faces with her mouth and hands seemed to have a certain element of attachment in it.   The touches were often soft and caressing, and they were bestowed only on her especial friends, or on one or two strangers that she had taken at once into notable favor.   Once she leaned out of her baby carriage, calling and reaching to me, as if she wished to be taken ; but when I came to her, she wanted only to get hold of me, to put her hands and mouth softly on my face.

Up to about the middle of the month, in spite of her daily exercises with her toe, the baby had not altogether annexed her legs to

her conscious self and brought them under
her orders. She still had to hold the foot
forcibly with her hands all the time her toe
was in her mouth, or it would have kicked
away from her as if it was none of hers. It
is likely, too, that she had scarcely any idea
of those parts of her body which she could
not see and did not often touch. Indeed,
the psychologists tell us that we ourselves
have a decidedly inferior bodily consciousness in such parts — say between the shoulder blades. Even her own head must have
been mainly unknown territory to the baby
still, in spite of the curiosity she had felt
about it the month before. But now she
discovered by a chance touch that she could
investigate it with her hands, and proceeded
at once to do so, with a serious face.

In the latter half of the month, she went
a good deal farther toward getting a roughly
complete knowledge and control of her body.
She investigated her ear, her cheek, and the
back and sides of her head, from time to

time. She became quite expert in using legs
and hands, head and mouth, together, in getting hold of her toe. She sat alone longer
and longer, and by the end of the month
could have done so by the half hour, if she
had not always upset herself in five minutes
or so by turning and reaching about. She
had become very free in bending, squirming,
and changing her position when she lay on
the floor, and early in the third week of the
month she had turned clear over, from back
to stomach, in reaching after something.
She followed up the lesson at once, and soon
was rolling over whenever she wished — at
first having much ado to get her arm disen-
tangled from under her, but managing it
nicely before long.

It is possible she would have begun creeping at this time but for the impediment of
her clothes. She did stumble once upon almost the right movement, in trying to get
forward to something she wanted ; but her
feet and knees became entangled in her

skirts, and she gave it up. A week later,
she was put into short skirts, but by that
time the ability to roll over had diverted her
mind from creeping.

Babies must lose a great deal of their normal activity through clothes. They are
retracing a stage of human history in which
clothes had no part, and this new element
must   hamper   the   repetition   immensely.
Clothes they must wear — they do not live
in tropic forests nor own hair coverings;
but we ought to leave the little limbs as free
as we can without risk from cold. A chance
to roll about nude in a room that is safely
warm is a great thing for a baby.

She did not again use any sign language
as advanced as when she had asked to be put
on the table; that incident was a sort of
herald of a later stage of development. But
in the latter part of the month her regular
means of communication were decidedly better developed than in the first part. She
would coax for a frolic by leaning forward

with an urgent " Oo ! oo ! " and expressive
movements of her body ; but if she was asking instead for an object she wished, or to be
taken into her mother's arms, there were
small but quite definite differences in tone,
expression, and movement, so that we usually
knew at once which she meant.

About a week before the end of the month
a great step toward intercommunication by
speech took place. We began to suspect
that the baby knew her own name, she turned
to look so often just after it had been spoken.
To test it I stood behind her, and in an ordinary tone accosted her as Bobby, Tom, Kitten, Mary, Jacob, Baby, and all sorts of other
names. Whenever I said Ruth, Toodles, or
Toots, she turned and looked expectantly at
me, but not at any other name. Now, Ruth
is our baby's proper name ; so it was evident
that she really did have some inkling of the
sound that meant her.

Not that she could rise yet to any such
abstract conception as that of a person or

of a name. But she had learned that this
sound was connected with interesting experiences — with frolics, and caresses, and trips
outdoors, with relief from discomforts, with
dinners, and all the other things that happened when people were attending to her.
It was out of such a beginning as this that
full understanding of articulate speech, in all
its logical intricacy, was to develop.

One of the most marked traits of the latter
weeks of this month was the surprising rapid-
ity with which things were grouping themselves in the baby's mind by association, in
a way that came nearer and nearer to definite
memory. She coaxed for a spoon, and when
she got it was still discontented, till we found
that she wished it to have milk in, as she
knew befitted a spoon — though for the milk
itself she did not care at all. She understood
what particular frolic was to be expected from
each of us. She turned, when she saw re-
flections, to look for the real object. She
made demonstrations of joy when she saw

her baby carriage, knowing well what it portended.

In two or three cases, there was at last unmistakable evidence of true memory, for at least a few minutes. For instance, in the last week of the month, sitting on her mother's lap, the baby caught sight of a knot of loops that adorned the centre of an ottoman close by, and reached her arms for it. By way of a joke on her, her mother set her on the ottoman. It was quite beyond the baby's sense of locality to divine what had become of the knot, and she looked all about her diligently to find it, leaning this way and that. By and by her mother took her back into her arms to nurse; but all the time she was nursing, she would stop now and then, sit up, and lean over to look for the lost knot.

At another time, when her mother came into the room with a new hat on, she reached out her hands for it with delight; her mother retreated at once, and put the hat safely out of sight, but when some minutes later the baby saw her again, her first look was at the top of her head, and seeing it now bare of lace and buttercups, she broke into a disappointed whimper.

All this time practice in her earlier attainments went vigorously on. She was watching, handling, reaching after things, all day long. Especially she watched all the movements of people; often, now, as they went in and out of doors, as they were seen through windows, came into sight or disappeared around corners. She must have been getting thus some idea of the way walls acted in shutting out her view, and of the relation of visible and invisible positions.

She had perhaps more troubles in this month than ever before, what with some fear of people, and the discomforts connected with her first pair of teeth, and also with the beginning of the weaning period. There were a number of days when her health and spirits were considerably depressed, and there was a good deal of fretting.   When the teeth were fairly through, and the insufficient food supplemented, her spirits came up with a bound, and she was more joyous than ever.

She had her first skin pain in this month — a scratched finger from a clasp on my shoulder — and wailed with vigor; yet it was forgotten in a few moments, and never thought of again.   It was evident that skin sensitiveness was still low, and that hurts left no after soreness.

It was about ten days before the end of the month that she first showed a decided emotional dependence on her mother.   She had been separated from her for some time (by a tedious dentist's engagement), had become hungry and sleepy, and had been frightened by an abrupt stranger.   At last she settled into a pitiful, steady crying — stopping at every angle in the corridor where I walked with her, and watching eagerly till it was turned, then breaking out anew when her mother did not prove to be around the corner. This tragic experience left a much deeper mark than the physical woes, and for some days the baby watched her mother rather anxiously, as if she feared she might lose her again unless she kept her eyes constantly upon her.

And so she was come to the end of her first half year. The breathing automaton had become an eager and joyous little being, seeing and hearing and feeling much as we do, knowing her own body somewhat, and controlling it throughout to a certain extent, laughing and frolicking, enjoying the vision of the world with a delicious zest, clinging to us not so much for physical protection as for human companionship, beginning to show a glimmer of intelligence, and to cross over with sign and sound the abyss between spirit and spirit.

X

BEGINNINGS OF LOCOMOTION

WHEN a baby has learned to see things clearly, and has known the joys of handling them, it is natural that he should soon come to feel the need of getting to them when they chance to lie beyond arm reach. Apparently the first impulse to move the whole body does always come from this desire to get at something; but I doubt if this remains a very important motive throughout the whole process of learning. There is so much in that process that is instinctive that the baby seems to be in great part taken up and carried on by a current of blind impulse. Then, too, the whole structure of bone, and joint, and muscle is so fitted to certain positions and movements that in the mere chance exercising of his limbs he is steadily brought nearer to the great race acts of balance and locomotion.

One might suppose that with babies sprawling, creeping, and toddling on every hand, we should not lack evidence on the beginnings of human locomotion ; but as a matter of fact, the stage that precedes walking is involved in a good deal of confusion. Records are scanty, and children seem to vary a good deal in their way of going at the thing. Most of them " creep before they gang " ; but there seems to be a stage before creeping, when, if the child is given full freedom of movement, he will get over the floor in some cruder way, rolling, hitching, dragging himself by the elbows, humping forward measure-worm fashion, or wriggling along like a snake. Perhaps, as I have already suggested, this is because skirts delay the natural beginning of creeping, and these other movements require less freedom of the legs ; perhaps there is some deeper reason connected with race history. Sometimes the baby makes these less efficient movements answer till walking is acquired, and never creeps at all.

Our baby, as we have seen, had already made her first ineffective attempts to pull herself forward and reach something; and lying face down, unable to turn over, had so propped herself with hands and knees that when she tried to move she almost stumbled on creeping unawares. But soon after she was six months old, she discovered the other half of the trick of rolling — reversing herself from front to rear as well as from rear to front; and this gave her such an enlarged freedom that it stopped all aspirations in other directions.

She did not deliberately turn over and over to get anywhere. She simply rolled and kicked about the floor, turning over when she felt like it or when she wished to reach something, highly content, and asking odds of nobody. If by chance she turned in the same direction a number of times in succession, she would drift halfway across the room, meeting no end of interesting things by the way — mamma's slipper tips, chair rockers, table legs, waste basket, petals dropped from the vases, and so on. It was a great enlargement of life, and kept her happy for six or seven weeks.

During this time, her balance in sitting grew .secure, so that she could sit on the floor as long as she chose, occupied with playthings; but she cared more for the rolling.

It was in these weeks, too, that two great new interests came into our baby's life. The first was a really passionate one, and it seized her suddenly, the week after she was half a year old. The door had just opened to admit a guest, amid a bustle of welcome, when a cry of such desire as we had never heard from our baby in all her little life called our attention to her. Utterly indifferent to the arrival of company (she who had always loved a stir of coming and going, and taken more interest in people than in anything else!) she was leaning and looking out of the window at the dog, as if she had never seen him before — though he had been before her eyes all her life. She would think of nothing else; the guest, expert in charming babies, could not get a glance.

Day after day, for weeks, the little thing was filled with excitement at sight of the shaggy Muzhik, moving her arms and body, and crying out with what seemed intensest joy and longing. When he came near, her excitement increased, and she reached out and caught at him; her face lighted with happiness when he stood close by; she showed not the least fear when he put his rough head almost in her face, but gazed earnestly at it; she watched for him at the window, or from her baby carriage. No person or thing had ever interested her so much. Muzhik, on his part, soon learned to give the snatching little hands a wide berth; and his caution may have enhanced his charm.

Later in the month, she showed somewhat similar excitement at sight of a cow. About the same time, too, she first noticed the pigeons as they flew up from the ground.

This was the beginning of a lasting interest in animals, animal pictures, animal stories. It is not easy to account fully for this interest, appearing in such intense degree, at so early an age. All children show it to some extent, though in many it is mingled with a good deal of fear. One is tempted to connect both the fear and the interest with race history — the intimate association of primitive man with animals; but a six-month baby is traversing a period of development far earlier than that of the primitive hunter. Professor Sully has some good suggestions about the sympathy between children and animals, but these, too, fail of application to a baby so young. Probably to her the main charm was the movement, the rough resemblance to people, joined with so many differences, now first noticed with the interest of novelty — and (as later incidents made me suspect) the quantity of convenient hair to be pulled.

The other new interest waked late in the seventh month: that joy in outdoors that was for many months of the little one's life her best happiness.   Up to this time, she had liked to be taken out in her baby carriage, but mainly for the motion.   Now, one morning, grandma took her and sat down quietly on the veranda, saying that she wanted her to learn to love the sunshine, the birds and flowers and trees, without needing the baby carriage and its motion.   The little one sat in her lap, looking about with murmurs of delight; and after that, her happiness in rolling about freely was much greater when we spread a blanket on veranda or lawn, and laid her there.   Within two weeks, she would coax to be taken outdoors, and then coax till she was put down out of arms, and left to her own happiness.   She would roll about by the hour, the most contented baby in the world, breaking occasionally into cries and movements of overflowing joy.

I did not think that at this age the novel sights and sounds outdoors had much to do with her pleasure; she did not yet notice them much. Nor could it have been the wideness and freedom of outlook, for she had not yet come to distant seeing — a hundred feet was as far as I had ever seen her look. Later, all this counted; but now I thought that the mere physical effect of activity in the fresh air, together with the bright light, and perhaps the moving and playing of lights in the leaves, must make up most of the charm.

In the early weeks of the seventh month the baby's rollicking spirits were striking; in fact, she became for a time quite a little rowdy, ho-ho-ing and laughing in loud, rough tones, snatching this way and that, clutching at our hair with exultant shouts and clamor. In the latter part of the month, her manners were better — indeed, it was fully a year before I saw them as bad again; but she was much given to seizing at our faces, flinging herself at them with cries and growls (exactly as if she had been playing bear), and mouthing and lightly biting them. And indeed it must be confessed that while our baby's behavior was often very pretty for weeks together, she had many fits of rough play and hoydenish spirits, and our faces and hair were never quite safe from romping attacks before she was two years old. This boisterousness was not overflowing spirits (real joyousness showed itself more gently) and I could never trace its psychological origin.

At intervals during the month, she continued to improve her bodily knowledge of herself, investigating her head and face and even the inside of her mouth, with her fingers; she rubbed her forefinger curiously with her thumb; she ran out her tongue and moved it about, trying its motions and feeling her lips. And the very first day of the month there had appeared that curious behavior that we call "archness" and "coquetting" in a baby (though anything so grown up as real archness or coquetry is impossible at this age), looking and smiling at a person who was somewhat strange, but very amusing, to her, then ducking down her head when he spoke, and hiding her face on her mother's shoulder. Whatever the real reason of such behavior may be, there is plainly self-consciousness in it. So, too, when, at seven months old, she began to try deliberately to attract the interest of callers, wrinkling up her nose with a friendly grimace till they paid attention to her.

Both these forms of self-consciousness were common after this. Neither is what we could call human or rational self-consciousness. Any dog or kitten will show them. But they certainly are something more than mere bodily feeling of self. If we need a name for it, we might call it a beginning of *intelligent self-perception*, as distinguished both from

bodily self-feeling, and rational self-know-
ledge — in which the mind, years later, will
say to itself clearly, " This is *I*."

We now began to suspect (as she ended
her seventh month) that the baby was beginning to connect our names with us; and
when we tried her by asking, " Where is
grandpa ? " or " mamma " or " aunty," she
really did look at the right one often enough
to raise a presumption that she knew what
she was about.   The association of name
and person was still feeble and shaky, but it
proved to be real.   In a few days it was firm
as to grandpa (who was quite *persona grata*,
because he built up blocks for her to knock
down, and carried her about from object to
object, to let her touch and examine) ; and
in a week or two as to the rest of us.

Professor Preyer complains of teaching
babies mere tricks, which have no real relation to their development; and certainly it
is a sound rule that self-unfolding, not teaching, is the way in which a baby should

develop in the earliest years.   But Preyer's baby learned to wave his hand, and play "patacake," and show "How big is baby?" and the rest of it, just as other babies do; mammas and nurses cannot resist it.   And as long as the babies like it, I do not see that it can do any harm, if it is not overdone. Besides, it may be said that these standard tricks are all closely related to the sign language, and so fall in well with the natural development at this stage.   And again, the extreme teachability of the human child is his great superiority over the brute — all our civilization rests on it; and when the time comes that he is capable of receiving training, it may be as well that his power of doing so should be used a little, and that these simple gesture tricks of immemorial nursery tradition are good exercises to begin with.   It is possible to make a fetich of "self-development," beyond all common sense.

At all events, as our baby approached seven months old, her mamma had begun to teach her to wave by-by. For a couple of weeks, the mother would hold up the little hand and wave it at the departing guest, and before long the baby would give a feeble waggle or two after her mother had let go; next, she would need only to be started; and a week after she was seven months old she waved a spontaneous farewell as I left the room. There was a long history of the gesture after that, for it was lost and re-gained, confused with other hand tricks and straightened out, and altogether played a considerable part in the story of sign language and of memory, which I shall not have time to relate. But at all times it paid for itself in the delight it gave the baby: it re-conciled her to almost any parting, and even to going to bed.

Her objection to going to bed, which had been evident since the fifth month, was be-cause she thought sleeping was a waste of good playtime, not because she had any as-sociations of fear and repugnance connected with it. She had never been left to cry herself to sleep alone, but was rocked and sung to in good old fashion. But she did show signs at this time of timidity and distress in waking from sleep, clinging piteously to her mother and crying. She had waked and cried alone a number of times, and, as I have already said, she seemed to have formed some associations of fear in this way. But I think there were deeper reasons for the confused distress on waking, which from now until half way through the third year appeared at times.

I have spoken several times of the ease with which even we grown people lose our sense of personal identity; and changes in brain circulation make such confusions especially likely at first waking from sleep. With babies, whose feeling of identity is but insecurely established, this must be much more common; moreover, a baby's conditions of breathing are less regular than ours, and it is probable that as he comes out of sleep, and the circulation and respiration of the waking hours slowly reëstablish themselves, he has all sorts of queer, lost feelings. I was pretty sure, from our baby's behavior in the next two years, that she struggled back to the firm shores of waking consciousness through dark waters of confusion, and needed a friendly hand to cling to. This, I suspect, is the secret of the wild crying in the night, which doctors call "night terror": it is not terror, I think, but vague distress, increased by the darkness — loss of self, of direction, of all one's usual bodily feeling.

In these sensitive states attending sleep it is likely that some of the emotional conditions for life are formed, and the ties between mother and child knit firmest. My observation is that the one the baby loves most is the one that sleeps close by, that bends over him as he struggles confusedly back to waking, and steers him tenderly through the valley of the shadow of sleep; and next, the one that plays most patiently and observantly with him — not the one that feeds him.

In her absorption in her growing bodily activity, the baby had taken no marked steps in intellectual development, though in skill of handling, and in ability to understand what went on about her and put two and two together, she made steady progress. Early in the eighth month, some definite instances of this appeared. She showed a discreet preference at bedtime for anybody rather than her mother, and clung vigorously round my neck or her grandfather's when that messenger of fate came for her. She dropped things to watch them fall, with a persistent zeal and interest such as she had not shown in earlier experiments of the sort. She knew what it meant if one of us put a hat on, and pleaded with outstretched hands and springing motion to go too. Once she found that in moving a long stick she was moving some twigs at its farther end, and kept up the experiment with curiosity.

It was about this time — the first fortnight of the eighth month — that taste first became a source of pleasure to our baby. She had been given an experimental taste of several things before, but beyond the grimace of surprise (it looks like utmost disgust, but there seems no doubt that it really means surprise only) with which little babies greet new tastes, she had shown no great interest in them. Now, as nature's supply grew scant, she was introduced more seriously to several supplementary foods, and at least once rejoiced over the taste a good deal. Still, she was apt soon to tire of them, and on the whole taste did not at any time in her first year take a large place among her interests.

As the middle of the eighth month approached, it was evident that an advance in power of movement was coming. The baby was getting up on hands and knees again; she made daily a few aimless creeping movements; and in her bath she would draw herself to her knees, and partly to her feet, holding by the edge of the tub, and somewhat supported by the water. A few days later she drew herself forward a few inches, flat on her stomach, to get something. But she still did not catch the idea of creeping, and rolling remained her great pleasure for another fortnight.

In this fortnight, which brought our baby to eight months old, the rolling grew very rapid and free. She would now roll over and over in the same direction, not to get anywhere in particular (she never learned to use rolling for that purpose), but just for fun. She varied the exercise with the most lively kicking — heels raised in air and brought down together with astonishing vigor and zest ; and with twisting about and getting on hands and knees, or even on hands and feet, prattling joyously, and having a beautiful time all by herself, for as long as the authorities would leave her alone. I have no note or memory that she ever tired of it, or asked for attention or change; it was always some one else who interfered, because meal-time or nap-time or something had come.

In the last week of the month she learned to raise herself to a sitting position; and as she could now sit up or lie down at will, she tumbled about the floor with still more variety and enjoyment. In the same week she began to pull herself daily quite to her feet in the tub. It was an ordinary wooden wash-tub which was bridging the interval between her own outgrown one and the grown-up bath-tub; and she would stand, leaning her weight partly on her hands, on the edge of the tub, with her feet planted wide apart, quite on the opposite side, giving her a pretty secure base.

In this fortnight the baby's understanding of us and feeling of nearness to us were noticeably greater. Her attachment to her favorites was striking. She would cling to us with all the strength of her little arms, sometimes pressing her lips against our faces in a primitive sort of kiss. Her desire for our attention was intense — little arms stretched out, face full of desire, while she uttered urgent cries. Now and then she was entirely unwilling to eat a meal till the person she had set her heart on at the moment had yielded to her pleading, and come to sit close beside her, for company.

She understood one or two little directions — "by-by," and "patacake"; or, at least, associated them with the acts. She had some idea of what "No, no!" meant, and she knew perfectly that she must not keep paper or flower petals in her mouth, and after biting off a bit would put out her tongue, laughing, to have the forbidden scrap removed. And one day when I said to her, "Don't you want to come to aunty?" without any gesture, she surprised me by leaning forward and putting out her hands to me, exactly as if I had reached my arms out for her. She could not have understood the whole question, for she hardly understood words at all at the time; but she must have made out "come," and, putting it with "aunty," which she had known for weeks, got at my meaning.

On the day she was eight months old, at last, the baby half sprawled, half crept, forward to get something. The early, aimless stages of locomotion were over, and she was about to start in in good earnest to learn to creep and to stand.

XI

CREEPING AND STANDING

Now, at eight months old, began a fortnight of rapid development in movements, all branching out from the position on hands and knees which the baby often took as she sprawled on the floor.

First she hit on two ways of sitting up, beginning on hands and knees. One of them, in fact, had appeared in the last days of the preceding month. She would tilt over sidewise till she was half sitting, leaning on one hand, then straighten up, raising the hand — and there you are, sitting. The other way, a few days later, was to begin as before on hands and knees, separate the knees, and lift herself over backward till she was sitting, turning the legs out at the knee. No grown person but a contortionist could do it, for our hips have not enough play in the socket to carry the movement through the last inch or two ; but babies' joints are flexible. This became our baby's regular method, and the position it left her in — legs spread out before her, bent directly out at the knee — was her every-day one for many months. Most babies, I believe, sit monkey fashion — legs straight, with soles turned in.

Watching carefully, we were sure that the baby did not at first use either method intelligently; she wanted to sit up, and shifted and lifted her body, scolding with impatience, and never knowing whether she would bring up in the desired position or not, till she found herself by luck where she wanted to be. In a few days, however, the right movements were sifted out from the useless ones, and she sat up and lay down at will.

In the same early days of the ninth month, another movement came of experimenting while on hands and knees — a backward creeping, pushing with the hands. The baby at once tried to utilize it to get to people and things, and it was funny to hear her chattering with displeasure as she found herself borne off the other way — backing sometimes into the wall, and pushing helplessly against it, like a little locomotive that had accidentally got reversed. She soon gave up trying to get anywhere by this "crawfishing," however, and then she enjoyed it, merely as movement.

The only reason I have heard suggested for this curious back-action creeping (which is not uncommon just before real creeping) is that the baby's arms are stronger than the legs, and as a pushing movement with them is more natural than a stepping one, a backward impulse is given, which the baby, as a rule, resents with comical displeasure.

Next, from hands and knees the baby learned to rise to hands and feet; to kneel, and then to sit back on her heels; and to make sundry variations on these positions, such as kneeling on one knee and one foot, or sitting on one heel, with the other foot thrust out sidewise, propping her.

In spite of two or three chance forward steps, she was eight and a half months old before she hit at last on real creeping; then one day I saw her several times creep forward a foot or two, and presently she was rolling an orange about and creeping after it. I tried in vain to lure her more than a couple of feet, to come to me or to get a plaything; she would creep a step or two, then sit back on her heels and call me to take her. Until almost the end of this month, indeed, she would creep for but very short distances, and always to reach something, not for pleasure in the movement.

But while she fumbled in such chance fashion towards creeping, she was carried on towards standing by strong and evident instinct. She pulled herself up daily, not to reach anything, but from an overwhelming desire to get to her feet; and when she found

herself on them she rejoiced and triumphed.
At this stage she almost invariably used a
low object to pull up by, so that she could
lean over it, propping her weight with her
hands — or with one hand, as she grew more
confident. It was after the middle of the
month that she first drew herself up, her
knees shaking, by a chair, to reach a favorite plaything; but thereafter chairs became
her great " stand by," in a very literal sense.

In kneeling, too, she showed joy. She
could not keep her balance on her knees for
more than a few seconds, but while she did
she exulted in the exploit, and patted and
waved her hands in glee. Aside from standing and kneeling, her advances in movement
were made with a curious lack of intelligent
consciousness of what she was about, as well
as of clear, compelling instinct. She seemed
to progress by blind experimenting, selecting
gradually out of a medley of others the acts
and positions that were most useful and best
fitted to the structure of her joints and
muscles.

Many babies before this stage show the walking instinct quite clearly. If they are held from above, so that their soles press lightly on a flat surface, the legs will begin to make good stepping movements. Our baby had failed to make this response hitherto; in this fortnight, however, it appeared, very imperfectly and irregularly, but steadily better; and with another week she took great delight in the exercise.

Amid all these new movements, rolling rapidly declined and disappeared. The baby was absorbed in her new powers, and during the latter half of the month her joy in them was exquisite. She was a thing to remember for a lifetime as she played on a quilt spread on the lawn in the hot June days — sitting and looking about her with laughter and ejaculations of pleasure, gazing up with wonder and interest at the branches swaying in the warm breeze, watching the dog, creeping about and examining the grass with grave attention, pulling to her feet at our knees

as we sat by with our reading and sewing.
And when we let her take the benefit of the
warm weather, and creep about the floor
stripped to the inmost layer of garments,
arms and legs bare, she was at the height of
joy. She would go from one position to
another, sitting and kneeling, tumbling and
scrambling and creeping about in endless
content.

That she paid her price for all this in increased knowledge of pain I hardly need say.
From the time she began to roll freely, she
had collided with table legs and the like;
and from then until she could walk, bumps
and scratches and pinches were almost daily
experiences. Her early creeping was so awkward that she would lose her footing, so to
speak, and come down hard on her face, and
her later and quicker creeping brought colli-
sions; in standing by chairs she would lose
hold and topple over; and in investigating
rockers, window blinds, lids, and all manner
of things, she did not fail to get her fingers
hurt now and then, in spite of all vigilance.

In the main, she was surprisingly indifferent to these mishaps; even when the blow had reddened the skin, she would look sober only a minute, then, at a laugh and encouraging word, would smile and go on with her play. This was doubtless partly temperament: babies cry with nervous fright more than with the actual pain of a bump, and she was a baby of tranquil nerves. But her skin sensitiveness was probably still low.

With experience of pain, either her sensitiveness or her timidity grew, and she made more fuss than she did at first; and over some especially severe hurts she screamed with lusty good-will. Still, it was noticeable on the whole how little she was troubled in learning to balance and move about by the pains that strewed the way; and this, I think, must be the normal condition with healthy children.

I have spoken just now of the pride and joy that were shown over kneeling and standing. The joy, of course, was an old story:

we have seen that every stage of advancing power had been accompanied by lively pleasure. But this feeling of pride, this exultation in herself as actor, was a new emotion, and quite characteristic of the higher type of self-consciousness the baby had entered on at about seven months old, as I have already related. In going through her little hand movements, too, she showed much consciousness and pride, looking prettily into our faces for approval, as she patted or waved her hands.

As the baby now approached nine months old, there was an indescribable dawning appearance of comprehension about her — an air of understanding her surroundings and getting into touch with our minds. She watched our movements not merely with curiosity, but with an apparent attempt to interpret them, sometimes with a curious, puzzled drawing of the mouth that looked like mental effort. Many things she did interpret perfectly well: for instance, if I picked a rose and held it up, smiling, she knew that it was for her, and broke into jubilation accordingly. She volunteered to play peekaboo from early in the month, holding up a cloth, basket lid, or whatever she had at hand, before her face, and peeping out with smiles. She made intelligent little adaptations in her own actions, such as pulling at the tablecloth to bring to her a paper that lay on it.

She seemed, by the latter part of the month, to understand vaguely a good deal that was said to her, when it was accompanied with a gesture. If I said, "Kiss aunty," and offered my cheek, she would press her lips against it. She would look around to see if her mother shook her head with "No, no!" when she crept up to pull at the books on a low shelf. Her little list of accomplishments, waving and patting her hands, and so on, she would go through at the mere word, without any gesture.

One important development in the latter

part of the month was a little imitative cry, something like mewing, associated with the cats — important because of its bearing on the beginnings of language. It has long been a dispute whether language began with imitation of the sounds of nature, or with spontaneous ejaculations — " the bow-wow theory and the pooh-pooh theory," as they were scoffingly nicknamed early in the course of the discussion. Our baby may seem to have given the weight of her authority to the bow-wow theory, for this mewing cry did in fact slowly develop months later into a name for " cat," and might be called the first remote foreshadowing of a spoken word. But on the whole, with her and with other babies, the early stages of speech confirm the best recent opinion — namely, that language is a complex product, into which both imitation and ejaculation enter, with perhaps still other elements.

About a week before the baby was nine months old, some one looked up from dinner and saw her standing by a lounge, steadied only by one hand pressed against it, while she waved the other in exultant joy. Her father sprang and caught her as she toppled, then set her on her feet within the circuit of his arms, but without support, for a few seconds. Her legs shook, but she stood without fear, in high delight.

After this, her standing at chairs grew rapidly freer and bolder, and the support she needed was daily less. At nine months old, she was absorbed in the desire to stand. She would hold on with one hand and lean down to pick up things with confidence and freedom. In the first week of the tenth month, she even liked to pull herself up to her feet, then deliberately let go, come down sitting with a thud, and look up laughing and triumphant. She evidently thought the coming down quite as fine an exploit as the getting up.

By this time she crept freely and rapidly, laughing with pleasure as she did so. If she was laid on a blanket on the lawn, she no longer tumbled about contentedly within its area, but struck off across the grass, stopping to investigate carefully any plant or fallen leaf she came across. The medley of positions and movements had disappeared, and creeping and standing, as the fittest, had survived.

Within a week after she was nine months old, the baby began to get up to her feet by low objects, and then, instead of stooping over them, to abandon all support, straighten up, and stand alone for several seconds, greatly pleased with herself. Next she could stand a minute at a time, with such slight support as a fold of a gown in her hand, or in a corner, steadied only by her shoulders against the wall. She no longer plumped down to the floor, but lowered herself cleverly — once (in the second week of the month) without any support at all, having absent-mindedly let go of the chair. In a few days more, it was not uncommon for her to forget to hold on, and to stand a few seconds alone by a chair; and if she was at some one's knee, where she felt more confidence, she would let go on purpose, and try deliberately to stand alone.

Now began a period of diligent self-training in standing. As I sat on the grass and the baby played beside me, she would put her hands on my knee, lift herself to her feet, and balance on them as long as she could — seven seconds at the most, in the second week of the month, a quarter of a minute in the third, if her attention was called away from her own balance by some interesting sight. She would totter, stretch out her arms to recover her balance, circle with them just as we do (the movement must be highly instinctive), come down with a jolt and a peal of baby laughter, scramble to my knees, and up again. People are foolish to go to the matinée for amusement if they have a chance, instead, to sit flat on a lawn on a summer day, and assist at a baby's standing lessons.

In these days there was evident again an intangible but great increase in the little one's mental alertness, her eager curiosity in following our movements, her look of effort to understand, her growing clearness in grouping associations and interpreting what she saw.

Her handling of things had long developed into elaborate investigation, turning an object over and examining every side, poking her fingers into crevices, opening and shutting lids, turning over the leaves of books; and now she was no longer satisfied with investigating such objects as she came across by chance — she began to have a passion (which increased for weeks and months, and long made up a great part of her life) to go and find what there was to see. She crept to the window and stood at the low sill, to look out, beating the pane with her soft little hands and laughing in an ecstasy of delight if the dog wandered by. She crept into the hall and explored it, sitting down in each corner to take a survey, and to look up the walls above her. Her toys were neglected; she was impatient of being held in arms, and eager only to get to the floor and use her new powers. She crept happily about for hours from chair to chair, from person to person, getting to her feet at each, and setting herself cleverly down again; smiling and crowing at each success, and coming to us for applause and caresses. She did not want to leave the floor for her meals, and was reconciled to them only if she might stand at her mother's side and take her milk or porridge in small doses, interspersed with play. She ran away from us on hands and knees, laughing, if she thought we were about to pick her up.

Outdoors her happiness was even greater than in the month before, and her cries of rapture as she looked up, down, and around, and realized her own activity in the midst of all the waving and shining and blooming things, were remarkable — uttered, as it were, from the very deeps of her little soul, with that impassioned straining of the central muscles by which a baby throws such abandon of longing or ecstasy into his voice. We seem to have lost the vivid expressiveness of primitive cries in getting the precision and convenience of articulate words.

The sights and sounds of outdoors now contributed greatly to the little girl's joy there. She had for some weeks noticed sounds more than ever before — the tapping of a woodpecker, for instance, or the stamping of a horse in the stable — and now she was quick to look and listen at the note of a bird. She watched the birds, too, for the first time, as they flew from tree to tree; and the profuse California flowers were objects of incessant desire and pleasure.

The power of communication was considerably increased in this month by the acquisition of one exceedingly useful sign. The way in which it was developed is an interesting example of the evolution of such signs.

First the baby began to use her forefinger tip for specially close investigations; at the same time she had a habit of stretching out her hand towards any object that interested her — by association, no doubt, with touching and seizing movements. Combining these two habits, she began to hold her forefinger separate from the others when she thus threw out her hand towards an interesting object; then, in the second week of the month, she directed this finger alone towards what interested her; and by the third week, the gesture of pointing was fairly in use. She pointed to the woodshed door, with her mewing cry, when she wished to see the kittens; to the garden door, with pleading sounds, when she wished to be taken thither; to the special bush from which she wished a rose. She pointed in answer, instead of merely looking, when we asked, "Where is grandpa?" "Where is Muzhik?"

These questions can hardly have been understood, as questions; but it was more

than ever clear that she got some idea from
a good deal that we said, and now by the
words alone, without the help of gestures.
Doubtless she knew several simple words —
words of coming and going, of food, of the
kittens and the dog and the horse.

All this time she had shown no great
improvement in walking movements when
held from above, and she had no particular
ambition to walk.   But in the last week
of the month she began to edge along by
the side of a chair, holding to it — a great
advance.

The first attempts at climbing, too, appeared before she was quite ten months old.
In the third week of the tenth month the
baby had let herself down by her hands quite
cleverly from a large chair in which she had
been scrambling about — a feat that must
have been quite instinctive, since she did it
well and easily at the first try.   The last
day of the month, as she hovered at the foot
of the stairs (a region about which she had

much unsatisfied curiosity), some one helped her to put her knee on the lower step. Thereupon she laid hold on the next one, and pulled herself up, and with the same help, mounted two steps more. At this point her aunty's stereotyped appeal, " Don't help her! let her alone, and let me see what she will do!" prevailed. A candle was set on a higher step as a lure, and, sure enough, the little thing, unaided, set her knee on the higher level, laid hold with her hands, and drew herself up. It is significant that true climbing movements should be so early and so easily caught at a single partial lesson; and I shall have occasion to say more about it before the story of the baby's first year closes.

In the very last days of the tenth month came a wonderful spring upward in the little one's intelligence about her surroundings, and in her power of communicating with us. It involved the real beginning of spoken words — for the cat cry of the month before remained by itself, leading to nothing more, and though it was the first sound that expressed an idea, it was not from it, but from this later root, that spoken language sprang and grew.

But the mental and language progress of these few days, just as the baby came to ten months old, was the beginning of a stage of development that belonged to the later months — a beginning too important to be crowded in at the close of a chapter that is mainly concerned with movement development. So I keep the account of it for the story of the eleventh month.

XII

RUDIMENTS OF SPEECH ; CLIMBING AND PROGRESS TOWARD WALKING

> Talk before you go,
> Your tongue will be your overthrow,

says the old saw.   But perhaps our baby did not earn the ill omen, it was such a faint foreshadowing of speech that she was guilty of.   Probably she would not have been detected in it at all, had not ten months' practice made us pretty good detectives. Indeed, but for the notebook, by which I could compare from day to day the wavering approach to some meaning in her use of this or that syllable, I should not have dared to be sure there really was a meaning.   It is in these formless beginnings of a beginning that we get our best clues (as in all evolutionary studies) to the real secrets of the origin of language.

The little girl, as she came to ten months old, was a greater chatterer than ever, pouring out strings of meaningless syllables in joy or sorrow, with marvelous inflections and changes — such intelligent remarks as " Nĕnĕ-oom-bo," and " Ga-boo-ng," and " A-diddid-doo," and certain favored syllables over and over, such as " Dă-dă-dă."

In the last four days of the tenth month we began to suspect a faint consistency in the use of several of the most common sounds. We began to think that something like " Dă!" (varying loosely to " Gă!" or " Dng!" or " Did-dă!" or " Doo-doo!" but always hovering round plain " Dă!") was suspiciously often ejaculated when the little one threw out her hand in pointing, or exulted in getting to her feet; that " Nă-nănă!" was separating itself out as a wail of unwillingness and protest, and " Mă-mămă!" as a whimper of discontent, and loneliness, and desire of attention; while — nearest of all to a true word — a favorite old

murmur of " M-gm " or " Ng-gng " recurred
so often when something disappeared from
sight that we could not but wonder if we
had not here an echo of our frequent " All
gone ! "

All these sounds were used often enough
at other times, and other sounds were used
in their special places ; yet week by week
the notebook showed " Dă ! " growing into
the regular expression of discovering, pointing out, admiring, exulting ; " Nă-nă-nă ! "
into that of refusal and protest ; and " Mă-
mă-mă," which soon became " Mom-mom-
mom," into that of a special sort of wanting,
which slowly gathered itself about the mother
in particular.   I do not think that these were
echoes of our words " There ! " and " No ! "
and " Mamma ; " it was only slowly, and
after the baby was a year old, that they came
into unison with these words — and in the
case of " Mamma," not without some teaching.   It is more likely that we have here a
natural cry of pointing out, a natural nega-

tive, a natural expression of baby need and dependence, which give us a hint of the origin of our own words.

The fourth sound, however, which developed through many variations (such as "M-gâ," "Gâ," or "Gng") to a clear "Gông," "A-gông," and even "Gone," was plainly an echo. It was used as loosely as it was pronounced: the baby murmured "Ng-gng!" pensively when some one left the room; when she dropped something; when she looked for something she could not find; when she had swallowed a mouthful of food; when she heard a door close. She wounded her father's feelings by commenting "M-gâ!" as her little hands wandered about the unoccupied top of his head. She remarked "Gông!" when she slipped back in trying to climb a step; when she failed to loosen a cord she wished to play with; when she saw a portière, such as she was used to hide behind; when she was refused a bottle she had begged for. It meant disappearance, absence, failure, denial, and any object associated with these.

In just this fashion, Preyer's boy used his first word of human speech, at about this age. " Atta ! " the little fellow would murmur when some one left the room, or when the light went out — using a favorite old babble of his own, just as our baby did, to help him get hold of a grown-up word, " Adieu " or " Ta-ta," which carried the meaning he was after. The idea of *disappearance* — of the thing now seen, now gone — seems to take strong hold on babies very early ; I have known several other cases.

In all this we seem to see quite clearly the first steps in language making. The baby begins slowly to turn some of his commonest chattering sounds to special uses — not to carry thought to other people, but as mere exclamations to relieve his own mind. It was just twice within her first year that our baby turned to me when some one left the room, looked in my face, and said " Gông ! "

At all other times it was only murmured to herself. And most of the exclamations express a mood rather than a real idea; they are halfway between mere cries and words proper. Even when there is plainly an idea, as in "All gone," it is a big, vague blur of an idea, slowly taking form in the little mind, as the blurs of light and dark slowly outlined themselves into objects before the little eyes months before.

At this point the modern baby catches the trick of helping himself to our words ready made, and (though many glimpses of primitive speech show through the whole process of learning to talk) he thus saves himself in the main the long task of developing them, through which his ancestors toiled.

In fact, the next word our baby took into use, a fortnight later, was lifted bodily from our speech: a reproving "Kha!" by which we tried to disgust her with the state of her fingers after they had been plunged into apple sauce or like matters. She quite understood what it referred to, though she did not share our objection to messy fingers, and thereafter surveyed her own complacently in such plight, and commented, "Kha!" And I may here run ahead so far as to say that this was the full list of her spoken words within the first year, except that in the next month she used an assenting "Ĕ!" which may have been "Yes;" and in the last days of the year she began to exclaim first "By!" then "My!" (corrupted from "By-by") in saying farewell.

During this fortnight of swift language development the little one's progress in movements had been slight. But towards the middle of the eleventh month she took a fresh start. One day she raised herself to her feet without anything to hold to; stood on tiptoe to peer over the seat of her high chair; forgot to hold to me, in her eagerness for a fruit I was peeling, and stood alone for a minute and a half at least, while I peeled it and fed it into her mouth; clambered into

my lap (as I sat beside her on the floor), setting one little foot up first, laying hold of
my shoulder, and tugging herself up with
mighty efforts.

She chanced, too, on the art of shoving a
chair before her for a step or two; and the
next day, in her eagerness to reach a glass of
water her father was bringing, she took one
unconscious forward step, which ended in
prompt collapse on the lawn. But neither
of these beginnings was followed up by any
real advance in learning to walk. During
the rest of the month she edged about more
freely, and in the last week pushed chairs
before her a little again; and if we supported
her and urged her forward, she would walk
clumsily, much as a puppy will if you lead
him by the fore paws; but she seemed to
find the movement scarcely more natural
than the puppy does, and always wanted
soon to drop down to all-fours.

But climbing was a different matter.
Here the baby seemed laid hold of by strong

desire and instinct. The day after she climbed into my lap, she spent a long time zealously climbing up a doorstep and letting herself down backward from it. The day after that, she tackled the stairs and climbed two steps. Later in the day, I set her at the bottom of the stairs and moved slowly up before her. The little thing followed after (her mother's arms close behind, of course; no one would be crazy enough to start a baby upstairs without such precaution), tugging from step to step, grunting with exertion now and then, and exclaiming with satisfaction at each step conquered; slipping back once or twice, but undiscouraged — fifteen steps to the landing, where she pulled to her feet by the stair-post, hesitated, made a motion to creep down head first, then crept, laughing, across the landing, and up five steps more, and shouted with triumph to find herself on the upper floor. She even looked with ambition at the garret stairs, and started towards them; but an open door tempted her aside to explore a room, and she forgot the stairs.

For the rest of the month the baby dropped to hands and knees and scrabbled joyously for the stairs at every chance of open door; she was not satisfied without going up several times daily; and having people who believed in letting her do things, and insuring her safety by vigilance while she did them, instead of by holding her back, she soon became expert and secure in mounting. She made assaults, too, on everything that towered up and looked in the least climbable — boxes, chairs, and all sorts of things, quite beyond her present powers. She seemed possessed by a sort of blind compulsion towards the upward movement.

What are we to make of this strong climbing impulse, this untaught skill in putting up the foot or knee and pulling the body up, while walking is still unnatural? I sought out every record I could find, and the indications are that our baby was not an excep-

tion; that as a rule climbing does come before walking, if a baby is left free to develop
naturally.   Of course in many cases walking
is artificially hastened and climbing pre-
vented.

Can we help suspecting a period, somewhere in the remote ages, when the baby's
ancestry dwelt amid the treetops, and learned
to stand by balancing on one branch while
they held by a higher one? when they edged
along the branch, holding on above, but
dropped to all-fours and crept when they
came to the ground now and then to get
from tree to tree?   The whole history of
the baby's movements points to this: the
strong arms and clinging hands, from birth;
the intense impulse to *pull up*, even from the
beginning of sitting; the way in which standing always begins, by laying hold above and
pulling up; the slow and doubtful development of creeping, as if the ancestral creature
had been almost purely a tree-dweller, with
no period of free running on all-fours.

Tree-dwelling creatures, living on the dainties of the forest, fruit and nuts and eggs and birds, are better nourished than the ground-roaming tribes; but that is not half the story. The tree mothers cannot tuck their babies away in a lair and leave them; the tree babies cannot begin early to scramble about, like little cubs — their dwelling is too unsafe. There is nothing for it but the mother's arms; the baby must be held, and carried, and protected longer than the earth babies. That was the handicap of the tree life, our ancestors might have thought — the helpless babies. But, as we have seen in an earlier chapter, it was that long, helpless babyhood that gave the brain its chance to grow and made us human.

At eleven months old our little girl could stand alone as long as she cared to, though perhaps it was not till the next month that she felt altogether secure on her feet. She could climb up and down stairs with perfect ease. She could walk held by one hand, but she did not care to, and creeping was still her main means of getting anywhere.

Her understanding of speech had grown wonderfully, and as she was docile in obeying directions, I could always find out whether she knew a thing by name by saying, " Point to the rose," or " Bring the book to aunty," and thus found it possible to make out a trustworthy list of the words she knew: fifty-one names of people and things; twenty-eight action words, which she proved she understood by obeying (" give " and "sit down," and the like), and a few adverbial expressions, like " where " and " all gone " — eighty-four words in all, securely associated with ideas. She understood them in simple combinations, too, such as, " Bring mamma Ruth's shoes;" and often, where she did not know all the words in a sentence, she could guess quite shrewdly from those she did, interpreting our movements vigilantly.

For her own speech, the small set of spoken words she owned was of little use;

indeed, as I have said, these were only exclamations. For talking to us she used a wonderfully vivid and delicate language of grunts, and cries, and movements. She would point to her father's hat, and beg till it was given her; then creep to him and offer the hat, looking up urgently into his face, or perhaps would get to her feet at his side and try to put it on his head; when he put it on, up would go her little arms with pleading cries till he took her, and then she would point to the door and coax to be carried outdoors. She would offer a handkerchief with asking sounds when she wished to play peekaboo; or a whistle, to be blown; or a top, to be spun. When she was carried about the garden or taken driving, or when she crept exploring and investigating about the rooms, she would keep up a most dramatic running comment of interest, joy, inquiry, amusement, desire; and it was remarkable what shades of approval and disapproval, assent, denial, and request she could make perfectly clear.

XIII

WALKING ALONE; DEVELOPING INTELLI-GENCE

AND now our little girl was entered on the last month of the year — a month of the most absorbing activity, yet perhaps rather in practicing the powers she already had than in developing new ones. She added to the list of words she understood till it was impossible to make record of them all — new ones cropped up at every turn. She made the two small additions to her spoken words that I have already mentioned. She became perfectly secure in standing, and she was even more zealous to climb than before, making nothing, in the latter part of the month, of turning at the top of the stairs and sliding down, head first or feet first, rarely needing for safety the vigilant arms that always hovered ready to catch her.

For a time she made little advance towards walking, though she began now to show some pleasure and pride in being led about by the hand. But about the middle of the month the walking instinct seemed at last to stir. The little one had often stepped from chair to chair, keeping a hand on one till she had fairly hold of the other. If the gap was an inch wider than she could cross thus, she dropped down and crept. Now one day she looked at the tiny gap, let go her chair, stood longingly, made a movement as if to take the single step, and dropped ignominiously and crept; nor would she trust herself of her own accord to movement on her feet (though once her mother did coax her a few steps) for nearly a week. Then at last she ventured it.

I did not see the first exploit, but the next day I set her against the wall and told her to walk, and she would step forward with much sense of insecurity, tottering and taking tiny inches of steps, her legs spreading more widely at each one, till I caught her in my arms.   Once I let her go as far as she could. She would not give up and sit down, but went on as far as her legs would carry her, tremulous, pleased, half afraid, half proud, and wholly conscious of doing something remarkable; and when at the seventh step she subsided to the floor, she was not in the least frightened, but got up readily and tottered on another six steps.

The next day she had weakened, however, and for several days she would not try again; and when she did try, she fell down after a single step.   She wanted to try again, and crept back to the wall, stood up, laughed, waved her arms, made a false start, and could not quite find the courage.   In the four days that remained of her first year she sometimes forgot herself and took a step or two; and she was perfectly able to take half a dozen any time, strong and steady on her feet; but it was not till shortly after the close of the year that she cast aside her fears and suddenly was toddling everywhere.

It was about the middle of the twelfth month that the little one added the useful sign of nodding to her means of communicating. She had been taught to nod as a mere trick the month before, and took to it at once, jerking her whole little body at every nod and priding herself mightily on it. Perhaps because of this pride and pleasure, it became after a time a sort of expression of approval: she greeted us with nodding in sign of pleasure when we came in; she nodded like a mandarin when she heard she was to go to ride. So now, when a pleasant suggestion was made, "Would Ruth like a cracker?" "Does Ruth want to go see the kitties?" her nod of approval soon passed into the meaning of assent; indeed, it began now to be joined with the grunt of "Ĕ!" that I have mentioned. She had a perfectly intelligible negative grunt, too, just such as grumpy grown people use, out of the primitive stock of their remotest ancestry, no doubt.

I was nearly taken in at one time by this cheerful nodding and " Ĕ ! "   The little lady used them so intelligently when she was offered something she wanted, and refused so consistently when offered what she knew she did not want, that I began to set down any question as understood if she said yes to it.   But presently I had an inkling that when she did not know whether she wanted it or not, she said yes, on the chance — since most things prefaced by " Does Ruth want ? " proved pleasant.   So I asked her alluringly, " Does Ruth want a course in higher mathematics ? "

The rosy baby looked at me gravely, waited with a considering air, as she always did, taking it in, nodded gravely, and said decisively, " Ĕ ! "

" Does Ruth want to go and be a missionary in Raratonga ? "

" Ĕ ! " with no less decision.

I saved her confidence in my good faith by substituting something else as good, and more immediately practicable, for the mysterious attractions I had offered, and used due caution thereafter in recording her answers.

It was evident that in a primitive way the little one was comparing and inferring not a little by this time. A week before, her grandmother had told her which was O on a set of letter cards she played with, and presently she showed Q with an inquiring cry: "What is this that looks so much like O, and yet is not O?" It may be added that she always knew O afterwards, and picked up most of the other letters as easily — an evidence of the unnecessarily hard work we make of learning the letters by postponing them till the normal age of picking up the name of anything and everything is past.

She was, of course, sometimes quaintly misled in an inference by lack of knowledge. In the last week of the month I shut my eyes and asked her, "Where are aunty's eyes?" The baby tried in vain to find them behind the lids, and then leaned over from my lap and looked carefully for the lost eyes on the floor !

I hardly think that memory is much developed at this age ; the probability is that even the two year old remembers things only in glimpses — one here and one there, but nothing continuous : this is one of the great differences between his mind and ours. But our little girl plainly remembered some things for days. In the second week of the month her uncle showed her how he lifted the window sash, and four days after, catching sight of the finger handle, she tugged at it with impatient cries, trying to make the sash go up. A few days later, having a flower in her hand when her feet were bare, she began, with a sudden memory, to beg to have something done to her toes with it, and it proved that two or three weeks before her mother had stuck a flower between the fat toes.

All this month, even more than in the eleventh, she was incessantly busy in exploring and learning. She opened boxes, took things out, and put them back; worked with infinite diligence and seriousness at such matters as getting a rubber ring off a note-book I had stretched it round; investigated crannies, spaces under grates, doors ajar, with an undying curiosity.

She began to imitate our actions more: she tried to comb her hair, to put flowers into a vase, to mark on a paper with a pen-cil; she pulled at her toes and muttered, as if she were saying the piggy rhyme.

She had a distinct idea as to what con-stituted herself, and when she was asked, "Where is Ruth?" she did not indicate her whole body, but always seized her head in her hands with certainty and decision.

She took delight in the new uses of mind and memory, no less than in her bodily powers; she would recall the association of an object and its name with joyous laughter, and her "Dǎ!" when she was asked to point to something was a cry of pleasure.

She had not an atom of moral sense, nor the least capacity of penitence or pity, but she was a friendly little thing, with no worse tempers than a resentful whimpering when she was put into her clothes — incumbrances that she much disliked. She was assiduous in putting her crackers into her friends' mouths, whether for fun or for good-will; and it was not uncommon for her to throw herself, with kisses and clinging arms, about our necks after we had given her some specially valued pleasure, such as taking her outdoors. She was learning to coax effectively with kisses, too, when she wished very much to go.

And so the story of the swift, beautiful year is ended, and our wee, soft, helpless baby had become this darling thing, beginning to toddle, beginning to talk, full of a wide-awake baby intelligence, and rejoicing in her mind and body; communicating with us in a vivid and sufficient dialect, and overflowing with the sweet selfishness of baby coaxings and baby gratitude. And at a year old, there is no shadow on the charm from the perception that its end is near. By the second birthday we say, " Ah, we shall be losing our baby soon ! " But on the first, we are eager, as the little one herself is, to push on to new unfoldings; it is the high springtime of babyhood — perfect, satisfying, beautiful.